Jossey-Bass Teacher

Jossey-Bass Teacher provides K–12 teachers with essential knowledge and tools to create a positive and lifelong impact on student learning. Trusted and experienced educational mentors offer practical classroom-tested and theory-based teaching resources for improving teaching practice in a broad range of grade levels and subject areas. From one educator to another, we want to be your first source to make every day your best day in teaching. *Jossey-Bass Teacher* resources serve two types of informational needs—essential knowledge and essential tools.

Essential knowledge resources provide the foundation, strategies, and methods from which teachers may design curriculum and instruction to challenge and excite their students. Connecting theory to practice, essential knowledge books rely on a solid research base and time-tested methods, offering the best ideas and guidance from many of the most experienced and well-respected experts in the field.

Essential tools save teachers time and effort by offering proven, ready-to-use materials for in-class use. Our publications include activities, assessments, exercises, instruments, games, ready reference, and more. They enhance an entire course of study, a weekly lesson, or a daily plan. These essential tools provide insightful, practical, and comprehensive materials on topics that matter most to K–12 teachers.

Fantasy Basketball and Mathematics

Student Name: _____

Fantasy Sports and Mathematics Series

Fantasy Basketball and Mathematics

Student Workbook

Dan Flockhart

JOSSEY-BASS

Published by Jossey-Bass
A Wiley Imprint
989 Market Street, San Francisco, CA 94103-1741   www.josseybass.com

Jossey-Bass books and products are available through most bookstores. To contact Jossey-Bass directly, call our Customer Care Department within the U.S. at 800-956-7739, outside the U.S. at 317-572-3986, or fax 317-572-4002.

Jossey-Bass also publishes its books in a variety of electronic formats. Some content that appears in print may not be available in electronic books.

ISBN: 978-0-7879-9449-5

FIRST EDITION
PB Printing   10   9 8 7 6 5 4 3 2 1

About the Author

Dan Flockhart received his multiple-subject teaching credential from California State University, East Bay in 1988. He taught mathematics in grades 5 through 8 for eleven years at St. Matthew's Episcopal Day School in San Mateo, California, where he incorporated fantasy sports into his math curriculum. He has also taught general studies classes at College of the Redwoods in Eureka, California. He received a master of arts degree in education from Humboldt State University in 2005; the title of his thesis was "Teacher Perceptions of the Effects of Fantasy Football in the Teaching of Mathematics." Flockhart has enjoyed participating in fantasy sports for over twenty-five years.

In addition to authoring the Fantasy Sports and Mathematics series, Flockhart maintains a Web site, www.fantasysportsmath.com, where teachers can participate in forums and contests and find out more about the series.

Acknowledgments

I'd like to express my gratitude to Guy, who provided continual support and always lent his ear. I'm also grateful to all of the teachers who provided me with feedback. I am also thankful to Kate, who made all of this possible. You are one of my angels! I was also lucky to work with wonderful production editors, Elizabeth and Susan, and copyeditors, Carolyn and Bev. They were fun to work with and I was impressed with their willingness to do whatever it took to produce the best possible product. My thanks go out as well to Chris for creating one of the best covers I've ever seen. In addition, I'm grateful to Lena for ensuring that all the math is accurate. Finally, without the love and support I received from Tiffany and Annie, this project would not have made it to press.

To my boyhood heroes: Pistol Pete and Tiny Archibald,
the most exciting athletes this sports fan has ever seen;
Clyde, the Pearl, and Willis Reed, the leaders of my
beloved Knicks in the 1960s and 1970s; and Bob
McAdoo, whose sweet jumper I tried to emulate in vain.

Contents

Graphing Activities 123

Graphing 125

Practice Worksheets 131

Assessment 191

Fantasy Basketball and Mathematics Handouts

Description and Rules

Fantasy Basketball and Mathematics is a game in which you will draft and manage your own team of players from men's or women's professional, college, or high school basketball teams. Players earn points for rebounds, assists, steals, blocked shots, and points scored. Players lose points for fouls and turnovers. Each week, you will find the sum of the points earned by your players. The object of the game is to accumulate the highest number of points.

How to Select Players

There are two options for selecting players. Your teacher will decide which option your class will use.

Option 1: Permanent Teams with Salary Cap.
You have a salary cap of $25,000,000. This is the total amount you can spend on player values. Select eight professional players for the positions listed in Table 1. Your instructor will provide you with a list of players and their costs. It is not possible to select college or high school players with this option because player values are not accessible for college and high school players. Be aware that the Women's National Basketball Association season runs from June to September, which means that professional female players can be selected only by students who are in summer school. You may select a player even if another student has chosen the same one. Table 1 lists the number of players to be selected at each position as well as the number of players in a starting lineup for each position.

Option 2: Different Teams Each Week.
Each week, you will select one team. For example, if you live in Boston, you may decide to select your hometown professional team for the first week of the game. Perhaps you will choose college and high school teams from the Boston area for the second and third weeks, respectively. However, you will no longer be allowed to choose those teams in later weeks because each team can be selected only once by each student during the course of the game. However, other students are allowed

Table 1. Basketball Positions: Number to Be Selected and Number in a Starting Lineup

Position	Number to Be Selected	Number in Starting Lineup Each Week
Center	2	1
Forward	3	2
Guard	3	2

Description and Rules *(Cont'd.)*

to select those same teams, as long as each student selects a particular team only once during the course of the game. Consequently, two or more students can choose the same team in the same week. Unlike in option 1, you will compute points using team statistics rather than individual statistics. For example, if your team gets a total of 37 rebounds in a game, that number would be used to compute points.

If you use option 1 to select players, your roster of players will remain the same for the length of the game (unless you make a trade, which is explained in the next section, or if a player is declared injured and out for the season). If you use option 2, your players will change from week to week.

Trades

You may trade players with your classmates if you selected players using option 1. Trades do not have to be position for position; for example, you could trade a center for a forward. However, you should be able to field a full starting lineup each week. If you make a trade, it is important that you make the necessary changes to your fantasy team roster. Salary cap numbers do not apply to trades.

Injuries

If you cannot locate a player's name in the box scores, he or she is probably injured. *If this occurs, the player's score is counted as zero.* If a player is declared out for the year and if you used option 1 to select players, you may use the portion of the salary cap you spent on that player to purchase another player at the same position. A list of injured players can be found in newspapers as well as online at www.fantasysportsmath.com or on other sports Web sites.

Fantasy Team Roster

Name of Fantasy Team: _____   Team Owner: _____

Position	Name	Team	Cost
Center			
Center			
Forward			
Forward			
Forward			
Guard			
Guard			
Guard			
Total Cost			

How to Read Box Scores

Box scores are written in several formats, but they all convey the same basic information. A fabricated box score is shown in Table 1. The statistics you will use are highlighted in bold and include rebounds, assists, steals, turnovers, blocked shots, personal fouls, and points scored.

Table 1. Sample Box Score: Buzz at Hammer

Player	FG-A	FT-A	3P-A	Off	Reb	Ast	St	TO	Blk	PF	Pts
Buzz											
R. Yamamoto	1–5	0–0	1–4	2	4	2	1	0	0	2	5
B. Chow	6–9	4–4	0–0	1	10	3	0	4	3	3	16
N. Ozols	2–3	1–2	0–0	1	1	1	1	0	0	4	5
N. Williams	3–8	0–0	0–0	1	4	3	1	2	0	0	6
M. Johnson	4–8	4–6	1–3	0	1	1	2	2	0	2	15
O. Pommey	5–9	0–0	3–7	1	3	1	0	1	0	1	19
D. Jankowski	1–3	0–0	1–1	0	0	1	1	0	0	0	5
M. Brown	3–4	0–0	0–0	0	0	3	0	1	0	1	6
T. Markovic	0–5	0–0	2–5	0	0	0	0	0	0	1	6
Hammer											
U. Gomez	2–4	5–6	0–0	2	5	1	1	2	0	1	9
J. Miller	0–2	2–2	0–2	1	3	0	0	0	0	1	2
H. Jackson	5–8	7–11	0–0	1	8	0	1	4	1	4	17
J. Sokolov	1–4	0–0	0–0	0	2	4	0	1	1	0	2
L. Novak	4–10	4–5	2–2	0	3	4	1	3	0	2	18
A. Smith	4–4	3–6	0–0	0	0	0	1	2	3	2	11
J. Takahashi	2–5	1–2	1–2	1	6	1	0	0	0	2	8
G. Harris	1–2	0–0	0–0	1	1	5	1	3	1	2	2
V. Walker	9–14	0–0	2–5	1	2	1	5	4	0	3	24

Note: FG-A = field goals made and attempted; FT-A = free throws made and attempted; 3P-A = three-point shots made and attempted; Off = offensive rebounds; **Reb = rebounds; Ast = assists; St = steals; TO = turnovers; Blk = blocked shots; PF = personal fouls; Pts = points scored**. Items in bold will be used in the Fantasy Basketball and Math game.

How to Collect Data

Each week, you will use newspapers or online resources to collect data from one game in which each of your players in your starting lineup participated. You can choose the game that produced the best statistics for each player. Accessing data online is the quickest and easiest method. Statistics are also archived online so that you can still collect data if you have missed a week or two. To locate statistics online at www.fantasysportsmath.com, use the following steps:

a. Click the "Get Basketball Stats" link.

b. On the following page, use the calendar to select any day from the previous week.

c. Find a team one of your players participated in and click on the box score for that game. You can find the game during the previous week in which each of your players produced the best statistics.

Fantasy Basketball and Mathematics handouts

How to Compute Points

Table 1 lists the default scoring system, which includes two methods for computing points earned by your players. Your teacher will choose one of these methods for you to use and may have you compute points using additional scoring systems as well. The default scoring system can be used each week to determine the ranking of students' teams in the game. The default scoring system was designed so that you can plot the weekly points earned by your players to precise numerical values on stacked-bar and multiple-line graphs. This is explained later.

Table 2 lists the Huskies, a sample team that is used throughout this book. All players on the Huskies are from the box score in Handout 3. If you use option 1, all players on a

Table 1. Default Scoring System

Advanced Method	Basic Method	
For every	For every	Players earn
5 points	Point	$\dfrac{1}{36}$
5 rebounds	Rebound	$\dfrac{1}{9}$
3 blocked shots	Blocked shot	$\dfrac{1}{6}$
3 assists or steals*	Assist or steal	$\dfrac{1}{12}$
5 turnovers or fouls**	Turnover or foul	$-\dfrac{1}{18}$

*Any combination of assists or steals totaling three
**Any combination of turnovers or fouls totaling five

Table 2. The Huskies

Player	Position	Team
Nate Williams	Guard	Buzz
Tomas Markovic	Guard	Buzz
Lukas Novak	Forward	Hammer
Bobby Chow	Forward	Buzz
Hal Jackson	Center	Hammer

How to Compute Points *(Cont'd.)*

team will not usually be found in the same box score because you will normally select players from several teams.

Let's use the advanced method to compute the points earned by Hal Jackson, who scored 17 points. Players earn $\frac{1}{36}$ point for each set of 5 points scored. Points are not earned above multiples of five, so we round Jackson's 17 points down to the nearest multiple of five, which is 15. Since there are three fives in 15 and players earn $\frac{1}{36}$ point for each set of five points, Jackson earned $\frac{3}{36}$ point. This process is repeated with rebounds as well as turnovers/personal fouls; points are earned for each set of five. With respect to assists/steals and blocked shots, points are earned for each set of three, so we round down to the nearest multiple of three before dividing by three.

The points earned by individual players can be computed via two different methods: one uses algebra, while the other method does not. If you use both approaches to compute points, you can verify your results.

Tables 3 and 4 provide examples of how to compute points using the advanced method and the basic method, respectively.

Table 3. Computation of Weekly Points for Bobby Chow (Advanced Method)

Points scored:	16 points = 3 sets of 5	$3 \times \dfrac{1}{36} = \dfrac{3}{36}$
Rebounds:	10 rebounds = 2 sets of 5	$2 \times \dfrac{1}{9} = \dfrac{2}{9}$
Blocked shots:	3 blocked shots = 1 set of 3	$1 \times \dfrac{1}{6} = \dfrac{1}{6}$
Assists + steals:	3 assists/steals = 1 set of 3	$1 \times \dfrac{1}{12} = \dfrac{1}{12}$
Turnovers + fouls:	7 turnovers/fouls = 1 set of 5	$1 \times \left(-\dfrac{1}{18}\right) = -\dfrac{1}{18}$
Total points for Chow:		$\dfrac{18}{36} = \dfrac{1}{2}$

How to Compute Points *(Cont'd.)*

Table 4. Computation of Weekly Points for Bobby Chow (Basic Method)

Points scored:	16 points	$16 \times \dfrac{1}{36} = \dfrac{16}{36}$
Rebounds:	10 rebounds	$10 \times \dfrac{1}{9} = \dfrac{10}{9}$
Blocked shots:	3 blocked shots	$3 \times \dfrac{1}{6} = \dfrac{3}{6}$
Assists + steals:	3 assists/steals	$3 \times \dfrac{1}{12} = \dfrac{3}{12}$
Turnovers + fouls:	7 turnovers/fouls	$7 \times \left(-\dfrac{1}{18}\right) = -\dfrac{7}{18}$
Total points for Chow:		$\dfrac{69}{36} = 1\dfrac{11}{12}$

Fantasy Basketball and Mathematics handouts

Practice in Computing Points, Using the Default Scoring System

Ignore the third and fourth columns if you are using the basic method.

Jackson	Number	Number of Sets of 5	Number of Sets of 3	Multiplied by	Points Earned
Points scored			N/A	$\frac{1}{36}$	
Rebounds			N/A	$\frac{1}{9}$	
Blocked shots		N/A		$\frac{1}{6}$	
Assists + steals		N/A		$\frac{1}{12}$	
Turnovers + fouls			N/A	$-\frac{1}{18}$	
Total points					

Note: N/A = not applicable.

Chow	Number	Number of Sets of 5	Number of Sets of 3	Multiplied by	Points Earned
Points scored			N/A	$\frac{1}{36}$	
Rebounds			N/A	$\frac{1}{9}$	
Blocked shots		N/A		$\frac{1}{6}$	
Assists + steals		N/A		$\frac{1}{12}$	
Turnovers + fouls			N/A	$-\frac{1}{18}$	
Total points					

Note: N/A = not applicable.

Practice in Computing Points, Using the Default Scoring System *(Cont'd.)*

Markovic	Number	Number of Sets of 5	Number of Sets of 3	Multiplied by	Points Earned
Points scored			N/A	$\frac{1}{36}$	
Rebounds			N/A	$\frac{1}{9}$	
Blocked shots		N/A		$\frac{1}{6}$	
Assists + steals		N/A		$\frac{1}{12}$	
Turnovers + fouls			N/A	$-\frac{1}{18}$	
Total points					

Note: N/A = not applicable.

Novak	Number	Number of Sets of 5	Number of Sets of 3	Multiplied by	Points Earned
Points scored			N/A	$\frac{1}{36}$	
Rebounds			N/A	$\frac{1}{9}$	
Blocked shots		N/A		$\frac{1}{6}$	
Assists + steals		N/A		$\frac{1}{12}$	
Turnovers + fouls			N/A	$-\frac{1}{18}$	
Total points					

Note: N/A = not applicable.

Fantasy Basketball and Mathematics handouts

Practice in Computing Points, Using the Default Scoring System *(Cont'd.)*

Williams	Number	Number of Sets of 5	Number of Sets of 3	Multiplied by	Points Earned
Points scored			N/A	$\frac{1}{36}$	
Rebounds			N/A	$\frac{1}{9}$	
Blocked shots		N/A		$\frac{1}{6}$	
Assists + steals		N/A		$\frac{1}{12}$	
Turnovers + fouls			N/A	$-\frac{1}{18}$	
Total points					

Note: N/A = not applicable.

Total team points: _____

Default Total Points Equation

If you are using the default scoring system, you can use the equation shown on this sheet (the *default total points equation*). This equation uses the same numerical values as the default scoring system to assign points to the players.

$$\frac{1}{36}(P) + \frac{1}{9}(R) + \frac{1}{6}(B) + \frac{1}{12}(A + S) - \frac{1}{18}(T + F) = W$$

Advanced Method

P = number of points scored by one player, rounded down to the nearest multiple of 5, divided by 5

R = number of rebounds by one player, rounded down to the nearest multiple of 5, divided by 5

B = number of blocked shots by one player, rounded down to the nearest multiple of 3, divided by 3

$A + S$ = number of assists plus number of steals by one player, rounded down to the nearest multiple of 3, divided by 3

$T + F$ = number of turnovers plus fouls by one player, rounded down to the nearest multiple of 5, divided by 5

Basic Method

P = number of points scored by one player

R = number of rebounds by one player

B = number of blocked shots by one player

$A + S$ = number of assists and steals by one player

$T + F$ = number of turnovers and fouls by one player

Computing Points Using the Default Total Points Equation: Example of the Advanced Method

Bobby Chow

$$\frac{1}{36}(3) + \frac{1}{9}(2) + \frac{1}{6}(1) + \frac{1}{12}(1) - \frac{1}{18}(1) = \frac{18}{36} = \frac{1}{2}$$

Computing Points Using the Default Total Points Equation: Example of the Basic Method

Bobby Chow

$$\frac{1}{36}(16) + \frac{1}{9}(10) + \frac{1}{6}(3) + \frac{1}{12}(3) - \frac{1}{18}(7) = 1\frac{11}{12}$$

Practice in Computing Points, Using the Default Total Points Equation

Use the total points equation below and either the advanced method or the basic method tocompute points earned for the listed players from the Huskies.

$$\frac{1}{36}(P) + \frac{1}{9}(R) + \frac{1}{6}(B) + \frac{1}{12}(A + S) - \frac{1}{18}(T + F) = W$$

Player	Computation	Points
Williams		
Markovic		
Novak		
Chow		
Jackson		
Total team points: _____		

Weekly Scoring Worksheet (Week 1)

Your teacher will help you fill in the numerical values in the "Multiplied by" column. Then fill in the scores for each of your players. *Ignore the third and fourth columns if you are using the basic method.*

Guard #1	Number	Number of Sets of 5	Number of Sets of 3	Multiplied by	Points Earned
Points scored			N/A		
Rebounds			N/A		
Blocked shots		N/A			
Assists + steals		N/A			
Turnovers + fouls			N/A		
Total points					

Note: N/A = not applicable.

Guard #2	Number	Number of Sets of 5	Number of Sets of 3	Multiplied by	Points Earned
Points scored			N/A		
Rebounds			N/A		
Blocked shots		N/A			
Assists + steals		N/A			
Turnovers + fouls			N/A		
Total points					

Note: N/A = not applicable.

Fantasy Basketball and Mathematics handouts

Weekly Scoring Worksheet
(Week 1) *(Cont'd.)*

Forward #1	Number	Number of Sets of 5	Number of Sets of 3	Multiplied by	Points Earned
Points scored			N/A		
Rebounds			N/A		
Blocked shots		N/A			
Assists + steals		N/A			
Turnovers + fouls			N/A		
Total points					

Note: N/A = not applicable.

Forward #2	Number	Number of Sets of 5	Number of Sets of 3	Multiplied by	Points Earned
Points scored			N/A		
Rebounds			N/A		
Blocked shots		N/A			
Assists + steals		N/A			
Turnovers + fouls			N/A		
Total points					

Note: N/A = not applicable.

Weekly Scoring Worksheet
(Week 1) *(Cont'd.)*

Center	Number	Number of Sets of 5	Number of Sets of 3	Multiplied by	Points Earned
Points scored			N/A		
Rebounds			N/A		
Blocked shots		N/A			
Assists + steals		N/A			
Turnovers + fouls			N/A		
Total points					

Note: N/A = not applicable.

Total team points: _____

Fantasy Basketball and Mathematics handouts

Peer Signature: _____

Weekly Scoring Worksheet
(Week 2)

Your teacher will help you fill in the numerical values in the "Multiplied by" column. Then fill in the scores for each of your players. *Ignore the third and fourth columns if you are using the basic method.*

Guard #1	Number	Number of Sets of 5	Number of Sets of 3	Multiplied by	Points Earned
Points scored			N/A		
Rebounds			N/A		
Blocked shots		N/A			
Assists + steals		N/A			
Turnovers + fouls			N/A		
Total points					

Note: N/A = not applicable.

Guard #2	Number	Number of Sets of 5	Number of Sets of 3	Multiplied by	Points Earned
Points scored			N/A		
Rebounds			N/A		
Blocked shots		N/A			
Assists + steals		N/A			
Turnovers + fouls			N/A		
Total points					

Note: N/A = not applicable.

Weekly Scoring Worksheet
(Week 2) *(Cont'd.)*

Forward #1	Number	Number of Sets of 5	Number of Sets of 3	Multiplied by	Points Earned
Points scored			N/A		
Rebounds			N/A		
Blocked shots		N/A			
Assists + steals		N/A			
Turnovers + fouls			N/A		
Total points					

Note: N/A = not applicable.

Forward #2	Number	Number of Sets of 5	Number of Sets of 3	Multiplied by	Points Earned
Points scored			N/A		
Rebounds			N/A		
Blocked shots		N/A			
Assists + steals		N/A			
Turnovers + fouls			N/A		
Total points					

Note: N/A = not applicable.

Fantasy Basketball and Mathematics handouts

Weekly Scoring Worksheet
(Week 2) *(Cont'd.)*

Center	Number	Number of Sets of 5	Number of Sets of 3	Multiplied by	Points Earned
Points scored			N/A		
Rebounds			N/A		
Blocked shots		N/A			
Assists + steals		N/A			
Turnovers + fouls			N/A		
Total points					

Note: N/A = not applicable.

Total team points: _____

Weekly Scoring Worksheet (Week 3)

Your teacher will help you fill in the numerical values in the "Multiplied by" column. Then fill in the scores for each of your players. *Ignore the third and fourth columns if you are using the basic method.*

Guard #1	Number	Number of Sets of 5	Number of Sets of 3	Multiplied by	Points Earned
Points scored			N/A		
Rebounds			N/A		
Blocked shots		N/A			
Assists + steals		N/A			
Turnovers + fouls			N/A		
Total points					

Note: N/A = not applicable.

Guard #2	Number	Number of Sets of 5	Number of Sets of 3	Multiplied by	Points Earned
Points scored			N/A		
Rebounds			N/A		
Blocked shots		N/A			
Assists + steals		N/A			
Turnovers + fouls			N/A		
Total points					

Note: N/A = not applicable.

Fantasy Basketball and Mathematics handouts

Weekly Scoring Worksheet
(Week 3) *(Cont'd.)*

Forward #1	Number	Number of Sets of 5	Number of Sets of 3	Multiplied by	Points Earned
Points scored			N/A		
Rebounds			N/A		
Blocked shots		N/A			
Assists + steals		N/A			
Turnovers + fouls			N/A		
Total points					

Note: N/A = not applicable.

Forward #2	Number	Number of Sets of 5	Number of Sets of 3	Multiplied by	Points Earned
Points scored			N/A		
Rebounds			N/A		
Blocked shots		N/A			
Assists + steals		N/A			
Turnovers + fouls			N/A		
Total points					

Note: N/A = not applicable.

Weekly Scoring Worksheet
(Week 3) *(Cont'd.)*

Center	Number	Number of Sets of 5	Number of Sets of 3	Multiplied by	Points Earned
Points scored			N/A		
Rebounds			N/A		
Blocked shots		N/A			
Assists + steals		N/A			
Turnovers + fouls			N/A		
Total points					

Note: N/A = not applicable.

Total team points: _____

Fantasy Basketball and Mathematics handouts

Peer Signature: _____

Weekly Scoring Worksheet
(Week 4)

Your teacher will help you fill in the numerical values in the "Multiplied by" column. Then fill in the scores for each of your players. *Ignore the third and fourth columns if you are using the basic method.*

Guard #1	Number	Number of Sets of 5	Number of Sets of 3	Multiplied by	Points Earned
Points scored			N/A		
Rebounds			N/A		
Blocked shots		N/A			
Assists + steals		N/A			
Turnovers + fouls			N/A		
Total points					

Note: N/A = not applicable.

Guard #2	Number	Number of Sets of 5	Number of Sets of 3	Multiplied by	Points Earned
Points scored			N/A		
Rebounds			N/A		
Blocked shots		N/A			
Assists + steals		N/A			
Turnovers + fouls			N/A		
Total points					

Note: N/A = not applicable.

Fantasy Basketball and Mathematics handouts

Weekly Scoring Worksheet
(Week 4) *(Cont'd.)*

Forward #1	Number	Number of Sets of 5	Number of Sets of 3	Multiplied by	Points Earned
Points scored			N/A		
Rebounds			N/A		
Blocked shots		N/A			
Assists + steals		N/A			
Turnovers + fouls			N/A		
Total points					

Note: N/A = not applicable.

Forward #2	Number	Number of Sets of 5	Number of Sets of 3	Multiplied by	Points Earned
Points scored			N/A		
Rebounds			N/A		
Blocked shots		N/A			
Assists + steals		N/A			
Turnovers + fouls			N/A		
Total points					

Note: N/A = not applicable.

Fantasy Basketball and Mathematics handouts

Weekly Scoring Worksheet
(Week 4) *(Cont'd.)*

Center	Number	Number of Sets of 5	Number of Sets of 3	Multiplied by	Points Earned
Points scored			N/A		
Rebounds			N/A		
Blocked shots		N/A			
Assists + steals		N/A			
Turnovers + fouls			N/A		
Total points					

Note: N/A = not applicable.

Total team points: _____

Peer Signature: _____

Weekly Scoring Worksheet
(Week 5)

Your teacher will help you fill in the numerical values in the "Multiplied by" column. Then fill in the scores for each of your players. *Ignore the third and fourth columns if you are using the basic method.*

Guard #1	Number	Number of Sets of 5	Number of Sets of 3	Multiplied by	Points Earned
Points scored			N/A		
Rebounds			N/A		
Blocked shots		N/A			
Assists + steals		N/A			
Turnovers + fouls			N/A		
Total points					

Note: N/A = not applicable.

Guard #2	Number	Number of Sets of 5	Number of Sets of 3	Multiplied by	Points Earned
Points scored			N/A		
Rebounds			N/A		
Blocked shots		N/A			
Assists + steals		N/A			
Turnovers + fouls			N/A		
Total points					

Note: N/A = not applicable.

Fantasy Basketball and Mathematics handouts

Weekly Scoring Worksheet
(Week 5) *(Cont'd.)*

Forward #1	Number	Number of Sets of 5	Number of Sets of 3	Multiplied by	Points Earned
Points scored			N/A		
Rebounds			N/A		
Blocked shots		N/A			
Assists + steals		N/A			
Turnovers + fouls			N/A		
Total points					

Note: N/A = not applicable.

Forward #2	Number	Number of Sets of 5	Number of Sets of 3	Multiplied by	Points Earned
Points scored			N/A		
Rebounds			N/A		
Blocked shots		N/A			
Assists + steals		N/A			
Turnovers + fouls			N/A		
Total points					

Note: N/A = not applicable.

Weekly Scoring Worksheet
(Week 5) *(Cont'd.)*

Center	Number	Number of Sets of 5	Number of Sets of 3	Multiplied by	Points Earned
Points scored			N/A		
Rebounds			N/A		
Blocked shots		N/A			
Assists + steals		N/A			
Turnovers + fouls			N/A		
Total points					

Note: N/A = not applicable.

Total team points: _____

Fantasy Basketball and Mathematics handouts

Weekly Scoring Worksheet
(Week 6)

Your teacher will help you fill in the numerical values in the "Multiplied by" column. Then fill in the scores for each of your players. *Ignore the third and fourth columns if you are using the basic method.*

Guard #1	Number	Number of Sets of 5	Number of Sets of 3	Multiplied by	Points Earned
Points scored			N/A		
Rebounds			N/A		
Blocked shots		N/A			
Assists + steals		N/A			
Turnovers + fouls			N/A		
Total points					

Note: N/A = not applicable.

Guard #2	Number	Number of Sets of 5	Number of Sets of 3	Multiplied by	Points Earned
Points scored			N/A		
Rebounds			N/A		
Blocked shots		N/A			
Assists + steals		N/A			
Turnovers + fouls			N/A		
Total points					

Note: N/A = not applicable.

Fantasy Basketball and Mathematics handouts

Weekly Scoring Worksheet
(Week 6) *(Cont'd.)*

Forward #1	Number	Number of Sets of 5	Number of Sets of 3	Multiplied by	Points Earned
Points scored			N/A		
Rebounds			N/A		
Blocked shots		N/A			
Assists + steals		N/A			
Turnovers + fouls			N/A		
Total points					

Note: N/A = not applicable.

Forward #2	Number	Number of Sets of 5	Number of Sets of 3	Multiplied by	Points Earned
Points scored			N/A		
Rebounds			N/A		
Blocked shots		N/A			
Assists + steals		N/A			
Turnovers + fouls			N/A		
Total points					

Note: N/A = not applicable.

Fantasy Basketball and Mathematics handouts

Weekly Scoring Worksheet
(Week 6) *(Cont'd.)*

Center	Number	Number of Sets of 5	Number of Sets of 3	Multiplied by	Points Earned
Points scored			N/A		
Rebounds			N/A		
Blocked shots		N/A			
Assists + steals		N/A			
Turnovers + fouls			N/A		
Total points					

Note: N/A = not applicable.

Total team points: _____

Weekly Scoring Worksheet
(Week 7)

Your teacher will help you fill in the numerical values in the "Multiplied by" column. Then fill in the scores for each of your players. *Ignore the third and fourth columns if you are using the basic method.*

Guard #1	Number	Number of Sets of 5	Number of Sets of 3	Multiplied by	Points Earned
Points scored			N/A		
Rebounds			N/A		
Blocked shots		N/A			
Assists + steals		N/A			
Turnovers + fouls			N/A		
Total points					

Note: N/A = not applicable.

Guard #2	Number	Number of Sets of 5	Number of Sets of 3	Multiplied by	Points Earned
Points scored			N/A		
Rebounds			N/A		
Blocked shots		N/A			
Assists + steals		N/A			
Turnovers + fouls			N/A		
Total points					

Note: N/A = not applicable.

Weekly Scoring Worksheet
(Week 7) *(Cont'd.)*

Forward #1	Number	Number of Sets of 5	Number of Sets of 3	Multiplied by	Points Earned
Points scored			N/A		
Rebounds			N/A		
Blocked shots		N/A			
Assists + steals		N/A			
Turnovers + fouls			N/A		
Total points					

Note: N/A = not applicable.

Forward #2	Number	Number of Sets of 5	Number of Sets of 3	Multiplied by	Points Earned
Points scored			N/A		
Rebounds			N/A		
Blocked shots		N/A			
Assists + steals		N/A			
Turnovers + fouls			N/A		
Total points					

Note: N/A = not applicable.

Weekly Scoring Worksheet
(Week 7) *(Cont'd.)*

Center	Number	Number of Sets of 5	Number of Sets of 3	Multiplied by	Points Earned
Points scored			N/A		
Rebounds			N/A		
Blocked shots		N/A			
Assists + steals		N/A			
Turnovers + fouls			N/A		
Total points					

Note: N/A = not applicable.

Total team points: _____

Fantasy Basketball and Mathematics handouts

Peer Signature: _____

Weekly Scoring Worksheet
(Week 8)

Your teacher will help you fill in the numerical values in the "Multiplied by" column. Then fill in the scores for each of your players. *Ignore the third and fourth columns if you are using the basic method.*

Guard #1	Number	Number of Sets of 5	Number of Sets of 3	Multiplied by	Points Earned
Points scored			N/A		
Rebounds			N/A		
Blocked shots		N/A			
Assists + steals		N/A			
Turnovers + fouls			N/A		
Total points					

Note: N/A = not applicable.

Guard #2	Number	Number of Sets of 5	Number of Sets of 3	Multiplied by	Points Earned
Points scored			N/A		
Rebounds			N/A		
Blocked shots		N/A			
Assists + steals		N/A			
Turnovers + fouls			N/A		
Total points					

Note: N/A = not applicable.

Fantasy Basketball and Mathematics handouts

Weekly Scoring Worksheet
(Week 8) *(Cont'd.)*

Forward #1	Number	Number of Sets of 5	Number of Sets of 3	Multiplied by	Points Earned
Points scored			N/A		
Rebounds			N/A		
Blocked shots		N/A			
Assists + steals		N/A			
Turnovers + fouls			N/A		
Total points					

Note: N/A = not applicable.

Forward #2	Number	Number of Sets of 5	Number of Sets of 3	Multiplied by	Points Earned
Points scored			N/A		
Rebounds			N/A		
Blocked shots		N/A			
Assists + steals		N/A			
Turnovers + fouls			N/A		
Total points					

Note: N/A = not applicable.

Fantasy Basketball and Mathematics handouts

Weekly Scoring Worksheet
(Week 8) *(Cont'd.)*

Center	Number	Number of Sets of 5	Number of Sets of 3	Multiplied by	Points Earned
Points scored			N/A		
Rebounds			N/A		
Blocked shots		N/A			
Assists + steals		N/A			
Turnovers + fouls			N/A		
Total points					

Note: N/A = not applicable.

Total team points: _____

Weekly Scoring Worksheet (Week 9)

Your teacher will help you fill in the numerical values in the "Multiplied by" column. Then fill in the scores for each of your players. *Ignore the third and fourth columns if you are using the basic method.*

Guard #1	Number	Number of Sets of 5	Number of Sets of 3	Multiplied by	Points Earned
Points scored			N/A		
Rebounds			N/A		
Blocked shots		N/A			
Assists + steals		N/A			
Turnovers + fouls			N/A		
Total points					

Note: N/A = not applicable.

Guard #2	Number	Number of Sets of 5	Number of Sets of 3	Multiplied by	Points Earned
Points scored			N/A		
Rebounds			N/A		
Blocked shots		N/A			
Assists + steals		N/A			
Turnovers + fouls			N/A		
Total points					

Note: N/A = not applicable.

Fantasy Basketball and Mathematics handouts

Weekly Scoring Worksheet
(Week 9) *(Cont'd.)*

Forward #1	Number	Number of Sets of 5	Number of Sets of 3	Multiplied by	Points Earned
Points scored			N/A		
Rebounds			N/A		
Blocked shots		N/A			
Assists + steals		N/A			
Turnovers + fouls			N/A		
Total points					

Note: N/A = not applicable.

Forward #2	Number	Number of Sets of 5	Number of Sets of 3	Multiplied by	Points Earned
Points scored			N/A		
Rebounds			N/A		
Blocked shots		N/A			
Assists + steals		N/A			
Turnovers + fouls			N/A		
Total points					

Note: N/A = not applicable.

Weekly Scoring Worksheet
(Week 9) *(Cont'd.)*

Center	Number	Number of Sets of 5	Number of Sets of 3	Multiplied by	Points Earned
Points scored			N/A		
Rebounds			N/A		
Blocked shots		N/A			
Assists + steals		N/A			
Turnovers + fouls			N/A		
Total points					

Note: N/A = not applicable.

Total team points: _____

Fantasy Basketball and Mathematics handouts

Weekly Scoring Worksheet (Week 10)

Your teacher will help you fill in the numerical values in the "Multiplied by" column. Then fill in the scores for each of your players. *Ignore the third and fourth columns if you are using the basic method.*

Guard #1	Number	Number of Sets of 5	Number of Sets of 3	Multiplied by	Points Earned
Points scored			N/A		
Rebounds			N/A		
Blocked shots		N/A			
Assists + steals		N/A			
Turnovers + fouls			N/A		
Total points					

Note: N/A = not applicable.

Guard #2	Number	Number of Sets of 5	Number of Sets of 3	Multiplied by	Points Earned
Points scored			N/A		
Rebounds			N/A		
Blocked shots		N/A			
Assists + steals		N/A			
Turnovers + fouls			N/A		
Total points					

Note: N/A = not applicable.

Fantasy Basketball and Mathematics handouts

Weekly Scoring Worksheet
(Week 10) *(Cont'd.)*

Forward #1	Number	Number of Sets of 5	Number of Sets of 3	Multiplied by	Points Earned
Points scored			N/A		
Rebounds			N/A		
Blocked shots		N/A			
Assists + steals		N/A			
Turnovers + fouls			N/A		
Total points					

Note: N/A = not applicable.

Forward #2	Number	Number of Sets of 5	Number of Sets of 3	Multiplied by	Points Earned
Points scored			N/A		
Rebounds			N/A		
Blocked shots		N/A			
Assists + steals		N/A			
Turnovers + fouls			N/A		
Total points					

Note: N/A = not applicable.

Fantasy Basketball and Mathematics handouts

Weekly Scoring Worksheet
(Week 10) *(Cont'd.)*

Center	Number	Number of Sets of 5	Number of Sets of 3	Multiplied by	Points Earned
Points scored			N/A		
Rebounds			N/A		
Blocked shots		N/A			
Assists + steals		N/A			
Turnovers + fouls			N/A		
Total points					

Note: N/A = not applicable.

Total team points: _____

Weekly Scoring Worksheet (Week 11)

Your teacher will help you fill in the numerical values in the "Multiplied by" column. Then fill in the scores for each of your players. *Ignore the third and fourth columns if you are using the basic method.*

Guard #1	Number	Number of Sets of 5	Number of Sets of 3	Multiplied by	Points Earned
Points scored			N/A		
Rebounds			N/A		
Blocked shots		N/A			
Assists + steals		N/A			
Turnovers + fouls			N/A		
Total points					

Note: N/A = not applicable.

Guard #2	Number	Number of Sets of 5	Number of Sets of 3	Multiplied by	Points Earned
Points scored			N/A		
Rebounds			N/A		
Blocked shots		N/A			
Assists + steals		N/A			
Turnovers + fouls			N/A		
Total points					

Note: N/A = not applicable.

Fantasy Basketball and Mathematics handouts

Weekly Scoring Worksheet
(Week 11) *(Cont'd.)*

Forward #1	Number	Number of Sets of 5	Number of Sets of 3	Multiplied by	Points Earned
Points scored			N/A		
Rebounds			N/A		
Blocked shots		N/A			
Assists + steals		N/A			
Turnovers + fouls			N/A		
Total points					

Note: N/A = not applicable.

Forward #2	Number	Number of Sets of 5	Number of Sets of 3	Multiplied by	Points Earned
Points scored			N/A		
Rebounds			N/A		
Blocked shots		N/A			
Assists + steals		N/A			
Turnovers + fouls			N/A		
Total points					

Note: N/A = not applicable.

Weekly Scoring Worksheet
(Week 11) *(Cont'd.)*

Center	Number	Number of Sets of 5	Number of Sets of 3	Multiplied by	Points Earned
Points scored			N/A		
Rebounds			N/A		
Blocked shots		N/A			
Assists + steals		N/A			
Turnovers + fouls			N/A		
Total points					

Note: N/A = not applicable.

Total team points: _____

Fantasy Basketball and Mathematics handouts

Weekly Scoring Worksheet (Week 12)

Your teacher will help you fill in the numerical values in the "Multiplied by" column. Then fill in the scores for each of your players. *Ignore the third and fourth columns if you are using the basic method.*

Guard #1	Number	Number of Sets of 5	Number of Sets of 3	Multiplied by	Points Earned
Points scored			N/A		
Rebounds			N/A		
Blocked shots		N/A			
Assists + steals		N/A			
Turnovers + fouls			N/A		
Total points					

Note: N/A = not applicable.

Guard #2	Number	Number of Sets of 5	Number of Sets of 3	Multiplied by	Points Earned
Points scored			N/A		
Rebounds			N/A		
Blocked shots		N/A			
Assists + steals		N/A			
Turnovers + fouls			N/A		
Total points					

Note: N/A = not applicable.

Weekly Scoring Worksheet
(Week 12) *(Cont'd.)*

Forward #1	Number	Number of Sets of 5	Number of Sets of 3	Multiplied by	Points Earned
Points scored			N/A		
Rebounds			N/A		
Blocked shots		N/A			
Assists + steals		N/A			
Turnovers + fouls			N/A		
Total points					

Note: N/A = not applicable.

Forward #2	Number	Number of Sets of 5	Number of Sets of 3	Multiplied by	Points Earned
Points scored			N/A		
Rebounds			N/A		
Blocked shots		N/A			
Assists + steals		N/A			
Turnovers + fouls			N/A		
Total points					

Note: N/A = not applicable.

Fantasy Basketball and Mathematics handouts

Weekly Scoring Worksheet
(Week 12) *(Cont'd.)*

Center	Number	Number of Sets of 5	Number of Sets of 3	Multiplied by	Points Earned
Points scored			N/A		
Rebounds			N/A		
Blocked shots		N/A			
Assists + steals		N/A			
Turnovers + fouls			N/A		
Total points					

Note: N/A = not applicable.

Total team points: _____

Weekly Scoring Worksheet
(Week 13)

Your teacher will help you fill in the numerical values in the "Multiplied by" column. Then fill in the scores for each of your players. *Ignore the third and fourth columns if you are using the basic method.*

Guard #1	Number	Number of Sets of 5	Number of Sets of 3	Multiplied by	Points Earned
Points scored			N/A		
Rebounds			N/A		
Blocked shots		N/A			
Assists + steals		N/A			
Turnovers + fouls			N/A		
Total points					

Note: N/A = not applicable.

Guard #2	Number	Number of Sets of 5	Number of Sets of 3	Multiplied by	Points Earned
Points scored			N/A		
Rebounds			N/A		
Blocked shots		N/A			
Assists + steals		N/A			
Turnovers + fouls			N/A		
Total points					

Note: N/A = not applicable.

Weekly Scoring Worksheet
(Week 13) *(Cont'd.)*

Forward #1	Number	Number of Sets of 5	Number of Sets of 3	Multiplied by	Points Earned
Points scored			N/A		
Rebounds			N/A		
Blocked shots		N/A			
Assists + steals		N/A			
Turnovers + fouls			N/A		
Total points					

Note: N/A = not applicable.

Forward #2	Number	Number of Sets of 5	Number of Sets of 3	Multiplied by	Points Earned
Points scored			N/A		
Rebounds			N/A		
Blocked shots		N/A			
Assists + steals		N/A			
Turnovers + fouls			N/A		
Total points					

Note: N/A = not applicable.

Weekly Scoring Worksheet
(Week 13) *(Cont'd.)*

Center	Number	Number of Sets of 5	Number of Sets of 3	Multiplied by	Points Earned
Points scored			N/A		
Rebounds			N/A		
Blocked shots		N/A			
Assists + steals		N/A			
Turnovers + fouls			N/A		
Total points					

Note: N/A = not applicable.

Total team points: _____

Fantasy Basketball and Mathematics handouts

Weekly Scoring Worksheet (Week 14)

Your teacher will help you fill in the numerical values in the "Multiplied by" column. Then fill in the scores for each of your players. ***Ignore the third and fourth columns if you are using the basic method.***

Guard #1	Number	Number of Sets of 5	Number of Sets of 3	Multiplied by	Points Earned
Points scored			N/A		
Rebounds			N/A		
Blocked shots		N/A			
Assists + steals		N/A			
Turnovers + fouls			N/A		
Total points					

Note: N/A = not applicable.

Guard #2	Number	Number of Sets of 5	Number of Sets of 3	Multiplied by	Points Earned
Points scored			N/A		
Rebounds			N/A		
Blocked shots		N/A			
Assists + steals		N/A			
Turnovers + fouls			N/A		
Total points					

Note: N/A = not applicable.

Weekly Scoring Worksheet
(Week 14) *(Cont'd.)*

Forward #1	Number	Number of Sets of 5	Number of Sets of 3	Multiplied by	Points Earned
Points scored			N/A		
Rebounds			N/A		
Blocked shots		N/A			
Assists + steals		N/A			
Turnovers + fouls			N/A		
Total points					

Note: N/A = not applicable.

Forward #2	Number	Number of Sets of 5	Number of Sets of 3	Multiplied by	Points Earned
Points scored			N/A		
Rebounds			N/A		
Blocked shots		N/A			
Assists + steals		N/A			
Turnovers + fouls			N/A		
Total points					

Note: N/A = not applicable.

Fantasy Basketball and Mathematics handouts

Weekly Scoring Worksheet
(Week 14) *(Cont'd.)*

Center	Number	Number of Sets of 5	Number of Sets of 3	Multiplied by	Points Earned
Points scored			N/A		
Rebounds			N/A		
Blocked shots		N/A			
Assists + steals		N/A			
Turnovers + fouls			N/A		
Total points					

Note: N/A = not applicable.

Total team points: _____

Peer Signature: _____

Weekly Scoring Worksheet (Week 15)

Your teacher will help you fill in the numerical values in the "Multiplied by" column. Then fill in the scores for each of your players. *Ignore the third and fourth columns if you are using the basic method.*

Guard #1	Number	Number of Sets of 5	Number of Sets of 3	Multiplied by	Points Earned
Points scored			N/A		
Rebounds			N/A		
Blocked shots		N/A			
Assists + steals		N/A			
Turnovers + fouls			N/A		
Total points					

Note: N/A = not applicable.

Guard #2	Number	Number of Sets of 5	Number of Sets of 3	Multiplied by	Points Earned
Points scored			N/A		
Rebounds			N/A		
Blocked shots		N/A			
Assists + steals		N/A			
Turnovers + fouls			N/A		
Total points					

Note: N/A = not applicable.

Fantasy Basketball and Mathematics handouts

Weekly Scoring Worksheet
(Week 15) *(Cont'd.)*

Forward #1	Number	Number of Sets of 5	Number of Sets of 3	Multiplied by	Points Earned
Points scored			N/A		
Rebounds			N/A		
Blocked shots		N/A			
Assists + steals		N/A			
Turnovers + fouls			N/A		
Total points					

Note: N/A = not applicable.

Forward #2	Number	Number of Sets of 5	Number of Sets of 3	Multiplied by	Points Earned
Points scored			N/A		
Rebounds			N/A		
Blocked shots		N/A			
Assists + steals		N/A			
Turnovers + fouls			N/A		
Total points					

Note: N/A = not applicable.

Fantasy Basketball and Mathematics handouts

Weekly Scoring Worksheet
(Week 15) *(Cont'd.)*

Center	Number	Number of Sets of 5	Number of Sets of 3	Multiplied by	Points Earned
Points scored			N/A		
Rebounds			N/A		
Blocked shots		N/A			
Assists + steals		N/A			
Turnovers + fouls			N/A		
Total points					

Note: N/A = not applicable.

Total team points: _____

Fantasy Basketball and Mathematics handouts

Weekly Scoring Worksheet (Week 16)

Your teacher will help you fill in the numerical values in the "Multiplied by" column. Then fill in the scores for each of your players. *Ignore the third and fourth columns if you are using the basic method.*

Guard #1	Number	Number of Sets of 5	Number of Sets of 3	Multiplied by	Points Earned
Points scored			N/A		
Rebounds			N/A		
Blocked shots		N/A			
Assists + steals		N/A			
Turnovers + fouls			N/A		
Total points					

Note: N/A = not applicable.

Guard #2	Number	Number of Sets of 5	Number of Sets of 3	Multiplied by	Points Earned
Points scored			N/A		
Rebounds			N/A		
Blocked shots		N/A			
Assists + steals		N/A			
Turnovers + fouls			N/A		
Total points					

Note: N/A = not applicable.

Fantasy Basketball and Mathematics handouts

Weekly Scoring Worksheet
(Week 16) *(Cont'd.)*

Forward #1	Number	Number of Sets of 5	Number of Sets of 3	Multiplied by	Points Earned
Points scored			N/A		
Rebounds			N/A		
Blocked shots		N/A			
Assists + steals		N/A			
Turnovers + fouls			N/A		
Total points					

Note: N/A = not applicable.

Forward #2	Number	Number of Sets of 5	Number of Sets of 3	Multiplied by	Points Earned
Points scored			N/A		
Rebounds			N/A		
Blocked shots		N/A			
Assists + steals		N/A			
Turnovers + fouls			N/A		
Total points					

Note: N/A = not applicable.

Fantasy Basketball and Mathematics handouts

Weekly Scoring Worksheet
(Week 16) *(Cont'd.)*

Center	Number	Number of Sets of 5	Number of Sets of 3	Multiplied by	Points Earned
Points scored			N/A		
Rebounds			N/A		
Blocked shots		N/A			
Assists + steals		N/A			
Turnovers + fouls			N/A		
Total points					

Note: N/A = not applicable.

Total team points: _____

Weekly Scoring Worksheet (Week 17)

Your teacher will help you fill in the numerical values in the "Multiplied by" column. Then fill in the scores for each of your players. *Ignore the third and fourth columns if you are using the basic method.*

Guard #1	Number	Number of Sets of 5	Number of Sets of 3	Multiplied by	Points Earned
Points scored			N/A		
Rebounds			N/A		
Blocked shots		N/A			
Assists + steals		N/A			
Turnovers + fouls			N/A		
Total points					

Note: N/A = not applicable.

Guard #2	Number	Number of Sets of 5	Number of Sets of 3	Multiplied by	Points Earned
Points scored			N/A		
Rebounds			N/A		
Blocked shots		N/A			
Assists + steals		N/A			
Turnovers + fouls			N/A		
Total points					

Note: N/A = not applicable.

Weekly Scoring Worksheet
(Week 17) *(Cont'd.)*

Forward #1	Number	Number of Sets of 5	Number of Sets of 3	Multiplied by	Points Earned
Points scored			N/A		
Rebounds			N/A		
Blocked shots		N/A			
Assists + steals		N/A			
Turnovers + fouls			N/A		
Total points					

Note: N/A = not applicable.

Forward #2	Number	Number of Sets of 5	Number of Sets of 3	Multiplied by	Points Earned
Points scored			N/A		
Rebounds			N/A		
Blocked shots		N/A			
Assists + steals		N/A			
Turnovers + fouls			N/A		
Total points					

Note: N/A = not applicable.

Weekly Scoring Worksheet
(Week 17) *(Cont'd.)*

Center	Number	Number of Sets of 5	Number of Sets of 3	Multiplied by	Points Earned
Points scored			N/A		
Rebounds			N/A		
Blocked shots		N/A			
Assists + steals		N/A			
Turnovers + fouls			N/A		
Total points					

Note: N/A = not applicable.

Total team points: _____

Weekly Scoring Worksheet (Week 18)

Your teacher will help you fill in the numerical values in the "Multiplied by" column. Then fill in the scores for each of your players. *Ignore the third and fourth columns if you are using the basic method.*

Guard #1	Number	Number of Sets of 5	Number of Sets of 3	Multiplied by	Points Earned
Points scored			N/A		
Rebounds			N/A		
Blocked shots		N/A			
Assists + steals		N/A			
Turnovers + fouls			N/A		
Total points					

Note: N/A = not applicable.

Guard #2	Number	Number of Sets of 5	Number of Sets of 3	Multiplied by	Points Earned
Points scored			N/A		
Rebounds			N/A		
Blocked shots		N/A			
Assists + steals		N/A			
Turnovers + fouls			N/A		
Total points					

Note: N/A = not applicable.

Weekly Scoring Worksheet
(Week 18) *(Cont'd.)*

Forward #1	Number	Number of Sets of 5	Number of Sets of 3	Multiplied by	Points Earned
Points scored			N/A		
Rebounds			N/A		
Blocked shots		N/A			
Assists + steals		N/A			
Turnovers + fouls			N/A		
Total points					

Note: N/A = not applicable.

Forward #2	Number	Number of Sets of 5	Number of Sets of 3	Multiplied by	Points Earned
Points scored			N/A		
Rebounds			N/A		
Blocked shots		N/A			
Assists + steals		N/A			
Turnovers + fouls			N/A		
Total points					

Note: N/A = not applicable.

Fantasy Basketball and Mathematics handouts

Weekly Scoring Worksheet
(Week 18) *(Cont'd.)*

Center	Number	Number of Sets of 5	Number of Sets of 3	Multiplied by	Points Earned
Points scored			N/A		
Rebounds			N/A		
Blocked shots		N/A			
Assists + steals		N/A			
Turnovers + fouls			N/A		
Total points					

Note: N/A = not applicable.

Total team points: _____

Peer Signature: _____

Weekly Scoring Worksheet (Week 19)

Your teacher will help you fill in the numerical values in the "Multiplied by" column. Then fill in the scores for each of your players. *Ignore the third and fourth columns if you are using the basic method.*

Guard #1	Number	Number of Sets of 5	Number of Sets of 3	Multiplied by	Points Earned
Points scored			N/A		
Rebounds			N/A		
Blocked shots		N/A			
Assists + steals		N/A			
Turnovers + fouls			N/A		
Total points					

Note: N/A = not applicable.

Guard #2	Number	Number of Sets of 5	Number of Sets of 3	Multiplied by	Points Earned
Points scored			N/A		
Rebounds			N/A		
Blocked shots		N/A			
Assists + steals		N/A			
Turnovers + fouls			N/A		
Total points					

Note: N/A = not applicable.

Fantasy Basketball and Mathematics handouts

Weekly Scoring Worksheet
(Week 19) *(Cont'd.)*

Forward #1	Number	Number of Sets of 5	Number of Sets of 3	Multiplied by	Points Earned
Points scored			N/A		
Rebounds			N/A		
Blocked shots		N/A			
Assists + steals		N/A			
Turnovers + fouls			N/A		
Total points					

Note: N/A = not applicable.

Forward #2	Number	Number of Sets of 5	Number of Sets of 3	Multiplied by	Points Earned
Points scored			N/A		
Rebounds			N/A		
Blocked shots		N/A			
Assists + steals		N/A			
Turnovers + fouls			N/A		
Total points					

Note: N/A = not applicable.

Weekly Scoring Worksheet
(Week 19) *(Cont'd.)*

Center	Number	Number of Sets of 5	Number of Sets of 3	Multiplied by	Points Earned
Points scored			N/A		
Rebounds			N/A		
Blocked shots		N/A			
Assists + steals		N/A			
Turnovers + fouls			N/A		
Total points					

Note: N/A = not applicable.

Total team points: _____

Fantasy Basketball and Mathematics handouts

Peer Signature: _____

Weekly Scoring Worksheet (Week 20)

Your teacher will help you fill in the numerical values in the "Multiplied by" column. Then fill in the scores for each of your players. *Ignore the third and fourth columns if you are using the basic method.*

Guard #1	Number	Number of Sets of 5	Number of Sets of 3	Multiplied by	Points Earned
Points scored			N/A		
Rebounds			N/A		
Blocked shots		N/A			
Assists + steals		N/A			
Turnovers + fouls			N/A		
Total points					

Note: N/A = not applicable.

Guard #2	Number	Number of Sets of 5	Number of Sets of 3	Multiplied by	Points Earned
Points scored			N/A		
Rebounds			N/A		
Blocked shots		N/A			
Assists + steals		N/A			
Turnovers + fouls			N/A		
Total points					

Note: N/A = not applicable.

Weekly Scoring Worksheet
(Week 20) *(Cont'd.)*

Forward #1	Number	Number of Sets of 5	Number of Sets of 3	Multiplied by	Points Earned
Points scored			N/A		
Rebounds			N/A		
Blocked shots		N/A			
Assists + steals		N/A			
Turnovers + fouls			N/A		
Total points					

Note: N/A = not applicable.

Forward #2	Number	Number of Sets of 5	Number of Sets of 3	Multiplied by	Points Earned
Points scored			N/A		
Rebounds			N/A		
Blocked shots		N/A			
Assists + steals		N/A			
Turnovers + fouls			N/A		
Total points					

Note: N/A = not applicable.

Fantasy Basketball and Mathematics handouts

Weekly Scoring Worksheet
(Week 20) *(Cont'd.)*

Center	Number	Number of Sets of 5	Number of Sets of 3	Multiplied by	Points Earned
Points scored			N/A		
Rebounds			N/A		
Blocked shots		N/A			
Assists + steals		N/A			
Turnovers + fouls			N/A		
Total points					

Note: N/A = not applicable.

Total team points: _____

Weekly Scoring Worksheet (Week 21)

Your teacher will help you fill in the numerical values in the "Multiplied by" column. Then fill in the scores for each of your players. *Ignore the third and fourth columns if you are using the basic method.*

Guard #1	Number	Number of Sets of 5	Number of Sets of 3	Multiplied by	Points Earned
Points scored			N/A		
Rebounds			N/A		
Blocked shots		N/A			
Assists + steals		N/A			
Turnovers + fouls			N/A		
Total points					

Note: N/A = not applicable.

Guard #2	Number	Number of Sets of 5	Number of Sets of 3	Multiplied by	Points Earned
Points scored			N/A		
Rebounds			N/A		
Blocked shots		N/A			
Assists + steals		N/A			
Turnovers + fouls			N/A		
Total points					

Note: N/A = not applicable.

Fantasy Basketball and Mathematics handouts

Weekly Scoring Worksheet
(Week 21) *(Cont'd.)*

Forward #1	Number	Number of Sets of 5	Number of Sets of 3	Multiplied by	Points Earned
Points scored			N/A		
Rebounds			N/A		
Blocked shots		N/A			
Assists + steals		N/A			
Turnovers + fouls			N/A		
Total points					

Note: N/A = not applicable.

Forward #2	Number	Number of Sets of 5	Number of Sets of 3	Multiplied by	Points Earned
Points scored			N/A		
Rebounds			N/A		
Blocked shots		N/A			
Assists + steals		N/A			
Turnovers + fouls			N/A		
Total points					

Note: N/A = not applicable.

Fantasy Basketball and Mathematics handouts

Weekly Scoring Worksheet
(Week 21) *(Cont'd.)*

Center	Number	Number of Sets of 5	Number of Sets of 3	Multiplied by	Points Earned
Points scored			N/A		
Rebounds			N/A		
Blocked shots		N/A			
Assists + steals		N/A			
Turnovers + fouls			N/A		
Total points					

Note: N/A = not applicable.

Total team points: _____

Fantasy Basketball and Mathematics handouts

Weekly Scoring Worksheet (Week 22)

Your teacher will help you fill in the numerical values in the "Multiplied by" column. Then fill in the scores for each of your players. *Ignore the third and fourth columns if you are using the basic method.*

Guard #1	Number	Number of Sets of 5	Number of Sets of 3	Multiplied by	Points Earned
Points scored			N/A		
Rebounds			N/A		
Blocked shots		N/A			
Assists + steals		N/A			
Turnovers + fouls			N/A		
Total points					

Note: N/A = not applicable.

Guard #2	Number	Number of Sets of 5	Number of Sets of 3	Multiplied by	Points Earned
Points scored			N/A		
Rebounds			N/A		
Blocked shots		N/A			
Assists + steals		N/A			
Turnovers + fouls			N/A		
Total points					

Note: N/A = not applicable.

Fantasy Basketball and Mathematics handouts

Weekly Scoring Worksheet
(Week 22) *(Cont'd.)*

Forward #1	Number	Number of Sets of 5	Number of Sets of 3	Multiplied by	Points Earned
Points scored			N/A		
Rebounds			N/A		
Blocked shots		N/A			
Assists + steals		N/A			
Turnovers + fouls			N/A		
Total points					

Note: N/A = not applicable.

Forward #2	Number	Number of Sets of 5	Number of Sets of 3	Multiplied by	Points Earned
Points scored			N/A		
Rebounds			N/A		
Blocked shots		N/A			
Assists + steals		N/A			
Turnovers + fouls			N/A		
Total points					

Note: N/A = not applicable.

Fantasy Basketball and Mathematics handouts

Weekly Scoring Worksheet
(Week 22) *(Cont'd.)*

Center	Number	Number of Sets of 5	Number of Sets of 3	Multiplied by	Points Earned
Points scored			N/A		
Rebounds			N/A		
Blocked shots		N/A			
Assists + steals		N/A			
Turnovers + fouls			N/A		
Total points					

Note: N/A = not applicable.

Total team points: _____

Peer Signature: _____

Weekly Scoring Worksheet
(Week 23)

Your teacher will help you fill in the numerical values in the "Multiplied by" column. Then fill in the scores for each of your players. *Ignore the third and fourth columns if you are using the basic method.*

Guard #1	Number	Number of Sets of 5	Number of Sets of 3	Multiplied by	Points Earned
Points scored			N/A		
Rebounds			N/A		
Blocked shots		N/A			
Assists + steals		N/A			
Turnovers + fouls			N/A		
Total points					

Note: N/A = not applicable.

Guard #2	Number	Number of Sets of 5	Number of Sets of 3	Multiplied by	Points Earned
Points scored			N/A		
Rebounds			N/A		
Blocked shots		N/A			
Assists + steals		N/A			
Turnovers + fouls			N/A		
Total points					

Note: N/A = not applicable.

Fantasy Basketball and Mathematics handouts

Weekly Scoring Worksheet
(Week 23) *(Cont'd.)*

Forward #1	Number	Number of Sets of 5	Number of Sets of 3	Multiplied by	Points Earned
Points scored			N/A		
Rebounds			N/A		
Blocked shots		N/A			
Assists + steals		N/A			
Turnovers + fouls			N/A		
Total points					

Note: N/A = not applicable.

Forward #2	Number	Number of Sets of 5	Number of Sets of 3	Multiplied by	Points Earned
Points scored			N/A		
Rebounds			N/A		
Blocked shots		N/A			
Assists + steals		N/A			
Turnovers + fouls			N/A		
Total points					

Note: N/A = not applicable.

Weekly Scoring Worksheet
(Week 23) *(Cont'd.)*

Center	Number	Number of Sets of 5	Number of Sets of 3	Multiplied by	Points Earned
Points scored			N/A		
Rebounds			N/A		
Blocked shots		N/A			
Assists + steals		N/A			
Turnovers + fouls			N/A		
Total points					

Note: N/A = not applicable.

Total team points: _____

Fantasy Basketball and Mathematics handouts

Weekly Scoring Worksheet (Week 24)

Your teacher will help you fill in the numerical values in the "Multiplied by" column. Then fill in the scores for each of your players. *Ignore the third and fourth columns if you are using the basic method.*

Guard #1	Number	Number of Sets of 5	Number of Sets of 3	Multiplied by	Points Earned
Points scored			N/A		
Rebounds			N/A		
Blocked shots		N/A			
Assists + steals		N/A			
Turnovers + fouls			N/A		
Total points					

Note: N/A = not applicable.

Guard #2	Number	Number of Sets of 5	Number of Sets of 3	Multiplied by	Points Earned
Points scored			N/A		
Rebounds			N/A		
Blocked shots		N/A			
Assists + steals		N/A			
Turnovers + fouls			N/A		
Total points					

Note: N/A = not applicable.

Weekly Scoring Worksheet
(Week 24) *(Cont'd.)*

Forward #1	Number	Number of Sets of 5	Number of Sets of 3	Multiplied by	Points Earned
Points scored			N/A		
Rebounds			N/A		
Blocked shots		N/A			
Assists + steals		N/A			
Turnovers + fouls			N/A		
Total points					

Note: N/A = not applicable.

Forward #2	Number	Number of Sets of 5	Number of Sets of 3	Multiplied by	Points Earned
Points scored			N/A		
Rebounds			N/A		
Blocked shots		N/A			
Assists + steals		N/A			
Turnovers + fouls			N/A		
Total points					

Note: N/A = not applicable.

Fantasy Basketball and Mathematics handouts

Weekly Scoring Worksheet
(Week 24) *(Cont'd.)*

Center	Number	Number of Sets of 5	Number of Sets of 3	Multiplied by	Points Earned
Points scored			N/A		
Rebounds			N/A		
Blocked shots		N/A			
Assists + steals		N/A			
Turnovers + fouls			N/A		
Total points					

Note: N/A = not applicable.

Total team points: _____

Peer Signature: _____

Weekly Scoring Worksheet
(Week 25)

Your teacher will help you fill in the numerical values in the "Multiplied by" column. Then fill in the scores for each of your players. *Ignore the third and fourth columns if you are using the basic method.*

Guard #1	Number	Number of Sets of 5	Number of Sets of 3	Multiplied by	Points Earned
Points scored			N/A		
Rebounds			N/A		
Blocked shots		N/A			
Assists + steals		N/A			
Turnovers + fouls			N/A		
Total points					

Note: N/A = not applicable.

Guard #2	Number	Number of Sets of 5	Number of Sets of 3	Multiplied by	Points Earned
Points scored			N/A		
Rebounds			N/A		
Blocked shots		N/A			
Assists + steals		N/A			
Turnovers + fouls			N/A		
Total points					

Note: N/A = not applicable.

Fantasy Basketball and Mathematics handouts

Weekly Scoring Worksheet
(Week 25) *(Cont'd.)*

Forward #1	Number	Number of Sets of 5	Number of Sets of 3	Multiplied by	Points Earned
Points scored			N/A		
Rebounds			N/A		
Blocked shots		N/A			
Assists + steals		N/A			
Turnovers + fouls			N/A		
Total points					

Note: N/A = not applicable.

Forward #2	Number	Number of Sets of 5	Number of Sets of 3	Multiplied by	Points Earned
Points scored			N/A		
Rebounds			N/A		
Blocked shots		N/A			
Assists + steals		N/A			
Turnovers + fouls			N/A		
Total points					

Note: N/A = not applicable.

Fantasy Basketball and Mathematics handouts

Weekly Scoring Worksheet (Week 25) *(Cont'd.)*

Center	Number	Number of Sets of 5	Number of Sets of 3	Multiplied by	Points Earned
Points scored			N/A		
Rebounds			N/A		
Blocked shots		N/A			
Assists + steals		N/A			
Turnovers + fouls			N/A		
Total points					

Note: N/A = not applicable.

Total team points: _____

Fantasy Basketball and Mathematics handouts

Peer Signature: _____

Weekly Scoring Worksheet
(Week 26)

Your teacher will help you fill in the numerical values in the "Multiplied by" column. Then fill in the scores for each of your players. *Ignore the third and fourth columns if you are using the basic method.*

Guard #1	Number	Number of Sets of 5	Number of Sets of 3	Multiplied by	Points Earned
Points scored			N/A		
Rebounds			N/A		
Blocked shots		N/A			
Assists + steals		N/A			
Turnovers + fouls			N/A		
Total points					

Note: N/A = not applicable.

Guard #2	Number	Number of Sets of 5	Number of Sets of 3	Multiplied by	Points Earned
Points scored			N/A		
Rebounds			N/A		
Blocked shots		N/A			
Assists + steals		N/A			
Turnovers + fouls			N/A		
Total points					

Note: N/A = not applicable.

Weekly Scoring Worksheet
(Week 26) *(Cont'd.)*

Forward #1	Number	Number of Sets of 5	Number of Sets of 3	Multiplied by	Points Earned
Points scored			N/A		
Rebounds			N/A		
Blocked shots		N/A			
Assists + steals		N/A			
Turnovers + fouls			N/A		
Total points					

Note: N/A = not applicable.

Forward #2	Number	Number of Sets of 5	Number of Sets of 3	Multiplied by	Points Earned
Points scored			N/A		
Rebounds			N/A		
Blocked shots		N/A			
Assists + steals		N/A			
Turnovers + fouls			N/A		
Total points					

Note: N/A = not applicable.

Fantasy Basketball and Mathematics handouts

Weekly Scoring Worksheet
(Week 26) *(Cont'd.)*

Center	Number	Number of Sets of 5	Number of Sets of 3	Multiplied by	Points Earned
Points scored			N/A		
Rebounds			N/A		
Blocked shots		N/A			
Assists + steals		N/A			
Turnovers + fouls			N/A		
Total points					

Note: N/A = not applicable.

Total team points: _____

HANDOUT 10

Weekly Scoring Worksheet Using a Total Points Equation (Week 1)

Write the total points equation you are using in the box below. Next, compute the points for each of your players, using the chart.

Player	Computation	Points
Center		
Forward #1		
Forward #2		
Guard #1		
Guard #2		

Total team points: _____

Fantasy Basketball and Mathematics handouts

Peer Signature: _____

Weekly Scoring Worksheet Using a Total Points Equation (Week 2)

Write the total points equation you are using in the box below. Next, compute the points for each of your players, using the chart.

Player	Computation	Points
Center		
Forward #1		
Forward #2		
Guard #1		
Guard #2		

Total team points: _____

Weekly Scoring Worksheet Using a Total Points Equation (Week 3)

Write the total points equation you are using in the box below. Next, compute the points for each of your players, using the chart.

Player	Computation	Points
Center		
Forward #1		
Forward #2		
Guard #1		
Guard #2		

Total team points: _____

Fantasy Basketball and Mathematics handouts

Weekly Scoring Worksheet Using a Total Points Equation (Week 4)

Write the total points equation you are using in the box below. Next, compute the points for each of your players, using the chart.

Player	Computation	Points
Center		
Forward #1		
Forward #2		
Guard #1		
Guard #2		

Total team points: _____

Weekly Scoring Worksheet Using a Total Points Equation (Week 5)

Write the total points equation you are using in the box below. Next, compute the points for each of your players, using the chart.

Player	Computation	Points
Center		
Forward #1		
Forward #2		
Guard #1		
Guard #2		

Total team points: _____

Fantasy Basketball and Mathematics handouts

Weekly Scoring Worksheet Using a Total Points Equation (Week 6)

Write the total points equation you are using in the box below. Next, compute the points for each of your players, using the chart.

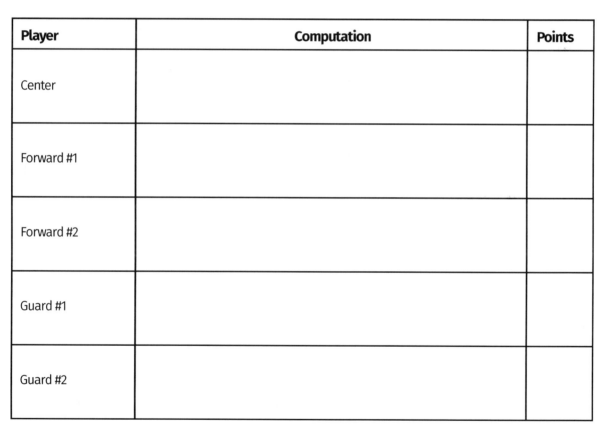

Player	Computation	Points
Center		
Forward #1		
Forward #2		
Guard #1		
Guard #2		

Total team points: _____

Weekly Scoring Worksheet Using a Total Points Equation (Week 7)

Write the total points equation you are using in the box below. Next, compute the points for each of your players, using the chart.

Player	Computation	Points
Center		
Forward #1		
Forward #2		
Guard #1		
Guard #2		

Total team points: _____

Fantasy Basketball and Mathematics handouts

Weekly Scoring Worksheet Using a Total Points Equation (Week 8)

Write the total points equation you are using in the box below. Next, compute the points for each of your players, using the chart.

Player	Computation	Points
Center		
Forward #1		
Forward #2		
Guard #1		
Guard #2		

Total team points: _____

Weekly Scoring Worksheet Using a Total Points Equation (Week 9)

Write the total points equation you are using in the box below. Next, compute the points for each of your players, using the chart.

Player	Computation	Points
Center		
Forward #1		
Forward #2		
Guard #1		
Guard #2		

Total team points: _____

Peer Signature: _____

Weekly Scoring Worksheet Using a Total Points Equation (Week 10)

Write the total points equation you are using in the box below. Next, compute the points for each of your players, using the chart.

Player	Computation	Points
Center		
Forward #1		
Forward #2		
Guard #1		
Guard #2		

Total team points: _____

Peer Signature: _____

Weekly Scoring Worksheet Using a Total Points Equation (Week 11)

Write the total points equation you are using in the box below. Next, compute the points for each of your players, using the chart.

Player	Computation	Points
Center		
Forward #1		
Forward #2		
Guard #1		
Guard #2		

Total team points: _____

Fantasy Basketball and Mathematics handouts

Weekly Scoring Worksheet Using a Total Points Equation (Week 12)

Write the total points equation you are using in the box below. Next, compute the points for each of your players, using the chart.

Player	Computation	Points
Center		
Forward #1		
Forward #2		
Guard #1		
Guard #2		

Total team points: _____

Weekly Scoring Worksheet Using a Total Points Equation (Week 13)

Write the total points equation you are using in the box below. Next, compute the points for each of your players, using the chart.

Player	Computation	Points
Center		
Forward #1		
Forward #2		
Guard #1		
Guard #2		

Total team points: _____

Fantasy Basketball and Mathematics handouts

Weekly Scoring Worksheet Using a Total Points Equation (Week 14)

Write the total points equation you are using in the box below. Next, compute the points for each of your players, using the chart.

Player	Computation	Points
Center		
Forward #1		
Forward #2		
Guard #1		
Guard #2		

Total team points: _____

Weekly Scoring Worksheet Using a Total Points Equation (Week 15)

Write the total points equation you are using in the box below. Next, compute the points for each of your players, using the chart.

Player	Computation	Points
Center		
Forward #1		
Forward #2		
Guard #1		
Guard #2		

Total team points: _____

Fantasy Basketball and Mathematics handouts

Peer Signature: _____

Weekly Scoring Worksheet Using a Total Points Equation (Week 16)

Write the total points equation you are using in the box below. Next, compute the points for each of your players, using the chart.

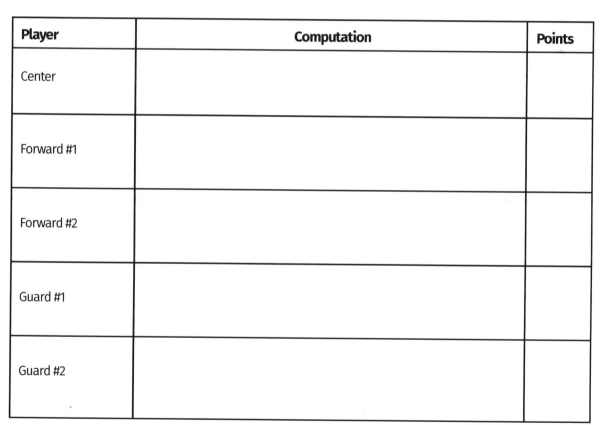

Player	Computation	Points
Center		
Forward #1		
Forward #2		
Guard #1		
Guard #2		

Total team points: _____

Weekly Scoring Worksheet Using a Total Points Equation (Week 17)

Write the total points equation you are using in the box below. Next, compute the points for each of your players, using the chart.

Player	Computation	Points
Center		
Forward #1		
Forward #2		
Guard #1		
Guard #2		

Total team points: _____

Peer Signature: _____

Weekly Scoring Worksheet Using a Total Points Equation (Week 18)

Write the total points equation you are using in the box below. Next, compute the points for each of your players, using the chart.

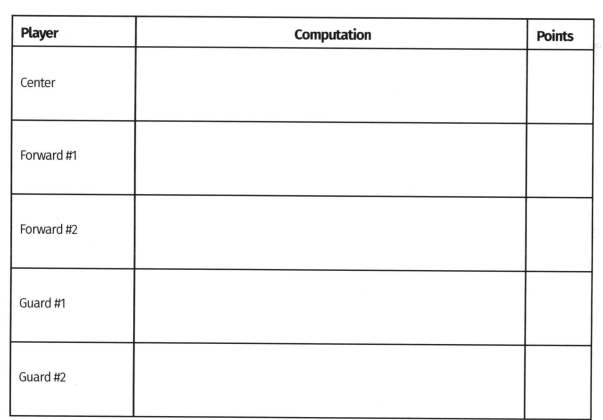

Player	Computation	Points
Center		
Forward #1		
Forward #2		
Guard #1		
Guard #2		

Total team points: _____

Peer Signature: _____

Weekly Scoring Worksheet Using a Total Points Equation (Week 19)

Write the total points equation you are using in the box below. Next, compute the points for each of your players, using the chart.

Player	Computation	Points
Center		
Forward #1		
Forward #2		
Guard #1		
Guard #2		

Total team points: _____

Copyright © 2007 by Dan Flockhart

Fantasy Basketball and Mathematics handouts

Weekly Scoring Worksheet Using a Total Points Equation (Week 20)

Write the total points equation you are using in the box below. Next, compute the points for each of your players, using the chart.

Player	Computation	Points
Center		
Forward #1		
Forward #2		
Guard #1		
Guard #2		

Total team points: _____

Weekly Scoring Worksheet Using a Total Points Equation (Week 21)

Write the total points equation you are using in the box below. Next, compute the points for each of your players, using the chart.

Player	Computation	Points
Center		
Forward #1		
Forward #2		
Guard #1		
Guard #2		

Total team points: _____

Fantasy Basketball and Mathematics handouts

Weekly Scoring Worksheet Using a Total Points Equation (Week 22)

Write the total points equation you are using in the box below. Next, compute the points for each of your players, using the chart.

Player	Computation	Points
Center		
Forward #1		
Forward #2		
Guard #1		
Guard #2		

Total team points: _____

Weekly Scoring Worksheet Using a Total Points Equation (Week 23)

Write the total points equation you are using in the box below. Next, compute the points for each of your players, using the chart.

Player	Computation	Points
Center		
Forward #1		
Forward #2		
Guard #1		
Guard #2		

Total team points: _____

Weekly Scoring Worksheet Using a Total Points Equation (Week 24)

Write the total points equation you are using in the box below. Next, compute the points for each of your players, using the chart.

Player	Computation	Points
Center		
Forward #1		
Forward #2		
Guard #1		
Guard #2		

Total team points: _____

Weekly Scoring Worksheet Using a Total Points Equation (Week 25)

Write the total points equation you are using in the box below. Next, compute the points for each of your players, using the chart.

Player	Computation	Points
Center		
Forward #1		
Forward #2		
Guard #1		
Guard #2		

Total team points: _____

Fantasy Basketball and Mathematics handouts

Weekly Scoring Worksheet Using a Total Points Equation (Week 26)

Write the total points equation you are using in the box below. Next, compute the points for each of your players, using the chart.

Player	Computation	Points
Center		
Forward #1		
Forward #2		
Guard #1		
Guard #2		

Total team points: _____

Total Points Week-by-Week

Team Name _____   Student Name _____

Week	Center	Forward #1	Forward #2	Guard #1	Guard #2	Weekly Total	Cumulative Total
1							
2							
3							
4							
5							
6							
7							
8							
9							
10							
11							
12							
13							
14							

Total Points Week-by-Week *(Cont'd.)*

Team Name _____   Student Name _____

Week	Center	Forward #1	Forward #2	Guard #1	Guard #2	Weekly Total	Cumulative Total
15							
16							
17							
18							
19							
20							
21							
22							
23							
24							
25							
26							

Fantasy Basketball and Mathematics handouts

Graphing Activities

Graphing

Each week, you will construct circle, stacked-bar, or multiple-line graphs.

Circle Graphs

Circle graphs indicate the percentage of a fantasy team's points earned by each player. The equation for computing the measurement of the central angle for a player's portion of the circle is as follows:

$$W \div S \times 360 = A$$

W = total weekly points for one player
S = total weekly points for the team
A = the measurement of the central angle of the circle graph

Figure 3.1. Circle Graph

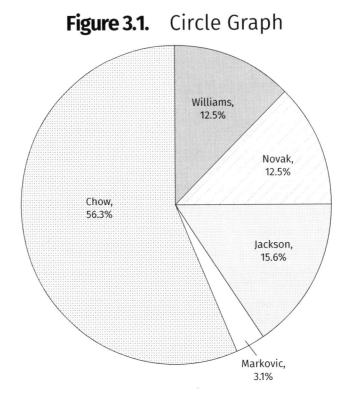

Huskies Scoring Breakdown, Week 1

Example Using the Advanced Method:

Jackson's total points for week 1: $\dfrac{5}{36}$

Total points for the Huskies for week 1: $\dfrac{8}{9}$

Step 1: $\dfrac{5}{36} \div \dfrac{8}{9} = \dfrac{5}{36} \cdot \dfrac{9}{8}$

Step 2: $\dfrac{5}{36} \cdot \dfrac{9}{8} = \dfrac{5}{32}$

Step 3: $\dfrac{5}{32} = .15625$

Step 4: $.15625 \cdot 360 = 56.25°$, which rounds to $56°$

Graphing

Stacked-Bar and Multiple-Line Graphs

Points earned by individual players can be shown on stacked-bar graphs and multiple-line graphs. A stacked-bar graph is a bar graph in which players' weekly points are "stacked" on top of each other. Multiple-line graphs are line graphs that depict the weekly points earned by two or more players. Examples of these graphs are found on the following pages. Each week, post your players' weekly points on stacked-bar and multiple-line graphs. Intervals of $\frac{2}{36}$ work well for the stacked-bar and multiple-line graphs if you are using the advanced method and the default scoring system. You may need to tape additional sheets of graph paper to the top of your first sheet to accommodate weeks in which your team scores significant points. The following pages contain examples of stacked-bar and multiple-line graphs.

Stacked-Bar Graph

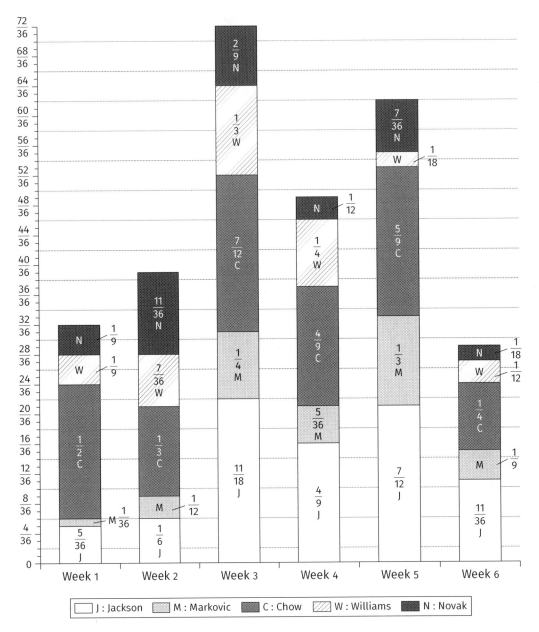

Huskies Scoring Breakdown, Weeks 1–6

Graphing

Multiple-Line Graph

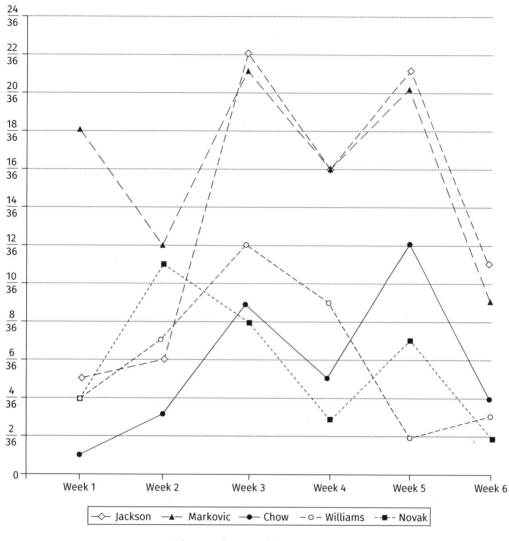

Huskies Scoring Breakdown, Weeks 1–6

Practice Worksheets

PRACTICE WORKSHEET 1

Rounding Whole Numbers and Expanded Notation

1. Round the following player salaries to the units given.

Salary	Nearest $10,000	Nearest $100,000	Nearest $1,000,000
$6,009,500	$6,010,000	$6,000,000	$6,000,000
$5,500,009			
$4,923,768			
$3,001,999			
$6,777,661			

2. Use expanded notation to represent the following player salaries.

Salary

$6,675,500 = 6,000,000 + 600,000 + 70,000 + 5,000 + 500

$6,009,500

$5,500,009

$4,923,768

$3,001,999

$2,999,000

Number sense

Name _____

Least Common Multiple
and Greatest Common Factor

Listed below are the points scored and rebounds by a player for the first 10 games of a season. Find the least common multiple and greatest common factor for each pair of numbers.

	Points Scored and Rebounds	Least Common Multiple	Greatest Common Factor
Games 1, 2	22, 11	22	11
Games 3, 4	19, 3		
Games 5, 6	30, 4		
Games 7, 8	32, 8		
Games 9, 10	45, 6		

Number sense

PRACTICE WORKSHEET 3

Operations with Whole Numbers

1. What is the difference in salary between the most expensive player and the least expensive player listed below?

Player A	$14,007,924
Player B	$13,950,351
Player C	$10,800,995
Player D	$12,675,228
Player E	$14,650,774
Player F	$3,777,902

2. What is the total cost of the players listed in problem 1?

3. What is the average cost of the players listed in problem 1, to the nearest dollar?

4. If John Ertola scored 273 points in 10 games, how many points did he average per game?

5. If 12 players each have a salary of $3.1 million, what is the sum of their salaries?

Number sense

Name _____

Equivalent Fractions

The points earned by individual players during week 8 are listed below. List the first three equivalent fractions for each.

1. Leslie White $\dfrac{5}{12}$ $\dfrac{10}{24}$ $\dfrac{15}{36}$ $\dfrac{20}{48}$

2. Kara Kolinsky $\dfrac{1}{9}$ _____ _____ _____

3. Melissa Williams $\dfrac{7}{36}$ _____ _____ _____

4. Kaneesha Harris $\dfrac{1}{4}$ _____ _____ _____

5. Ashley Walker $\dfrac{1}{6}$ _____ _____ _____

Number sense

PRACTICE WORKSHEET 5
Patterns and Multiples

(Use with Handout 12)

1. Find the first three multiples for the points earned (in 36ths) by Hal Jackson during week 6.

2. Find the first three multiples for the points earned (in 36ths) by Lukas Novak for week 5.

3. Find the first three multiples for the points earned (in 36ths) by Bobby Chow for week 3.

4. If $\frac{5}{12}$ is the fifth multiple of a number, what is the original number?

5. If 6 is the fourth multiple of a number, what is the original number?

Number sense

Name _____

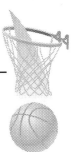

PRACTICE WORKSHEET 6

Ordering Fractions
and Decimals

(Use with Handout 12)

Example

For week 3, use inequalities to arrange the points earned by players on the Huskies in descending order.

$$\frac{22}{36} > \frac{21}{36} > \frac{12}{36} > \frac{9}{36} > \frac{8}{36}$$

After converting the fractions to decimals and rounding to the nearest thousandth, arrange the decimals in ascending order:

$$.222 < .250 < .333 < .583 < .611$$

For the following weeks, convert the points earned by the players on the Huskies to decimals. Then use inequalities to arrange the points earned in descending order. Round the decimals to the nearest thousandth.

Week 1

Week 2

Week 4

Week 5

Week 6

Number sense

PRACTICE WORKSHEET 7

Rounding Decimals

(Use with Handout 12)

Round each player's cumulative points from weeks 1–6 to the nearest tenth, hundredth, and thousandth.

Example

The cumulative points earned by Bobby Chow for weeks 1–6 were $\dfrac{96}{36} = 2\dfrac{24}{36} = 2.\overline{6}$

Round to the nearest tenth = 2.7

Round to the nearest hundredth = 2.67

Round to the nearest thousandth = 2.667

Table 1

Player	Total Points in Weeks 1–6 (Fraction)	Total Points in Weeks 1–6 (Decimal)	Nearest Tenth	Nearest Hundredth	Nearest Thousandth
Novak					
Williams					
Markovic					
Jackson					

In the following table, round the cumulative points for your players for weeks 1–6.

Table 2

Player	Total Points in Weeks 1–6 (Fraction)	Total Points in Weeks 1–6 (Decimal)	Nearest Tenth	Nearest Hundredth	Nearest Thousandth
Center					
Forward					
Forward					
Guard					
Guard					

Number sense

Name _____

Improper Fractions, Mixed Numbers, and Reciprocals

Some weekly point totals for the Huskies are listed below. Convert all improper fractions to mixed numbers, and write them in their simplest form.

Example

$$\frac{82}{36} = 2\frac{10}{36} = 2\frac{5}{18}$$

1. $\dfrac{97}{36}$

2. $\dfrac{32}{36}$

3. $\dfrac{66}{36}$

4. $\dfrac{120}{36}$

5. $\dfrac{48}{36}$

Write the reciprocals (in simplest form) of the original fractions given in items 1–5.

6.

7.

8.

9.

10.

Number sense

Adding and Subtracting Fractions

(Use with Handout 12)

Example

For week 5, find the sum of the points earned by Bobby Chow, Tomas Markovic, Lukas Novak, and Hal Jackson.

$$\frac{20}{36} + \frac{12}{36} + \frac{7}{36} + \frac{21}{36} = \frac{60}{36} = 1\frac{24}{36} = 1\frac{2}{3}$$

1. For week 3, find the sum of the points earned by Hal Jackson, Lukas Novak, and Nate Williams.

2. For week 2, find the sum of the points earned by all players except Hal Jackson and Lukas Novak.

3. For week 6, find the sum of the points earned by Hal Jackson, Tomas Markovic, and Lukas Novak.

4. For week 5, find the sum of the points earned by all players except Tomas Markovic and Nate Williams.

5. For week 4, find the sum of the points earned by all players except Hal Jackson and Bobby Chow.

Number sense

141

Stacked-Bar Graph

(Use with Handout 12)

Using graph paper, construct a stacked-bar graph for each week, based on the data below.
Hint: Convert all fractions so that they have a common denominator.

Player	Week 1	Week 2	Week 3
Serena Robinson	$\frac{11}{36}$	$\frac{1}{6}$	$\frac{1}{4}$
Vondra Davis	$\frac{1}{12}$	$\frac{7}{36}$	$\frac{7}{12}$
Gertrud Larlsson	$\frac{1}{18}$	$\frac{1}{2}$	$\frac{17}{36}$

Number sense

Multiplying and Dividing

Name _____

1. How many games would it take Karina Wallace to earn $1\frac{19}{36}$ points if she averaged $\frac{5}{36}$ points a game?

2. How many games would it take Denise Hackman to earn $2\frac{1}{4}$ points if she averaged $\frac{9}{36}$ point a game?

3. The product of the points earned by Kari Phelps and Stacey Underwood is $\frac{11}{144}$. If Phelps earned $\frac{11}{36}$ points, how many points did Underwood earn?

4. Frances Smith earned 10.5 points in 27 games. How many points did she earn per game, on average?

5. Fiona Shakelford earned $10\frac{5}{12}$ points. Connie Miller earned an average of $\frac{5}{12}$ points per week. How long would it take Miller to earn as many points as Shakelford?

Number sense   143

PRACTICE WORKSHEET 12

Rounding Fractions

(Use with Handout 12)

In Table 1, round players' cumulative points earned in weeks 1–6 to the nearest $\frac{1}{2}$, $\frac{1}{4}$, and $\frac{1}{8}$.

Example

Lukas Novak's cumulative points for weeks 1–6 $= \dfrac{35}{36}$

Round to the nearest $\dfrac{1}{2}$: 1

Round to the nearest $\dfrac{1}{4}$: 1

Round to the nearest $\dfrac{1}{8}$: 1

Table 1

	Total Points (Fraction)	Nearest $\frac{1}{2}$	Nearest $\frac{1}{4}$	Nearest $\frac{1}{8}$
Jackson				
Williams				
Markovic				
Chow				

Number sense

Rounding Fractions *(Cont'd.)*

In Table 2, round the cumulative points earned by your players in weeks 1–6.

Table 2

	Total Points (Fraction)	**Nearest $\frac{1}{2}$**	**Nearest $\frac{1}{4}$**	**Nearest $\frac{1}{8}$**
Center				
Forward				
Forward				
Guard				
Guard				

Multiplying and Dividing Decimals

1. During the last five years, a player had a player rating (a complex statistical ranking of his performance to date) of 78.64, 91.88, 86.75, 90.09, and 93.53. Find her average rating for the last five years.

2. A player works 8 hours a day, 195 days a year. Her salary is $6.4 million for one year. How much money does she make each working day? Each working hour? Each working minute? Each working second? In all cases, round your answers to the nearest cent.

3. If a snail can crawl at a rate of .07 feet per minute, how many hours will it take the snail to crawl the length of a basketball court (94 feet)? One mile?

4. If 30,000 fans each consumed an average of 6.75 ounces of soda at each game, how many ounces of soda were consumed in 15 games? How many 16-ounce sodas were consumed?

5. If a vendor selling ice cream sandwiches works three hours at $8.50 an hour and receives 45 cents for each sandwich sold, what is her income if she sold 223 sandwiches?

Number sense

PRACTICE WORKSHEET 14

Unit Rates

Example

At a basketball game, you can purchase 16 oz. of soda for $3.25 or 24 oz. for $4.20. Which size provides the lower price per ounce?

$$\$3.25 \div 16 \text{ oz.} = 20.3 \text{ cents per ounce}$$

$$\$4.20 \div 24 \text{ oz.} = 17.5 \text{ cents per ounce}$$

The 24-ounce size provides the lower price per ounce.

1. You can purchase 16 oz. of peanuts for $4.50 or 24 oz. for $5.75. What is the lower price per ounce?

2. If Monica Tillest drives her car 410 miles on 20 gallons of gas and Yu Yuan drives her car 450 miles on 23 gallons, what is the mileage (miles per gallon) for each car?

3. Ellen McGrady can purchase 40 acres of land for $3.5 million or 65 acres for $5.5 million. What is the lower price per acre?

4. Fans can purchase a season ticket (41 games) for $2,250, or they can buy a one-game ticket for $60. What is the lower price per game?

5. Which is higher per year: a salary of $6.5 million for 8 years or a salary of $11.5 million for 15 years?

Name _____

Converting Fractions, Decimals, and Percentages

(Use with Handout 12)

1. Find the cumulative points for weeks 1–6 for each player, and convert the fractions into decimals. Then round to the nearest tenth, hundredth, and thousandth. Finally, convert the decimal to a percentage, rounded to the nearest tenth.

	Total Points (Fraction)	Total Points (Decimal)	Rounded to Nearest Tenth	Rounded to Nearest Hundredth	Rounded to Nearest Thousandth	Percentage (Rounded to Nearest Tenth)
Chow	$2\frac{24}{36}$	$2.\overline{6}$	2.7	2.67	2.667	266.7%
Williams						
Novak						
Markovic						
Jackson						

2. Fill in the table below, using the cumulative points for the players on your team for the first six weeks.

Player	Total Points (Fraction)	Total Points (Decimal)	Rounded to Nearest Tenth	Rounded to Nearest Hundredth	Rounded to Nearest Thousandth	Percentage (Rounded to Nearest Tenth)
G						
G						
F						
F						
C						

Number sense

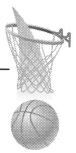

Ratios

(Use with Handout 12)

Example

For week 2, find the ratio of the total points earned by Nate Williams to the total points earned by Hal Jackson, and then convert this to a percentage.

$$\frac{7}{36} \div \frac{1}{6} = \frac{7}{36} \times \frac{6}{1}$$

$$\frac{7}{36} \times \frac{6}{1} = \frac{7}{6} = 1\frac{1}{6}$$

$$1\frac{1}{6} = 1.1\overline{6} = 1.17 = 117\%$$

For week 3, find the following ratios and convert them to percentages.

1. $\dfrac{\text{Total points earned by Nate Williams and Tomas Markovic}}{\text{Total points earned by Hal Jackson}}$

2. $\dfrac{\text{Total points earned by Lukas Novak and Bobby Chow}}{\text{Total points earned by Nate Williams and Tomas Markovic}}$

3. $\dfrac{\text{Total points earned by Hal Jackson}}{\text{Total points earned by Lukas Novak and Bobby Chow}}$

For week 5, find the following ratios and convert them to percentages:

4. $\dfrac{\text{Total points earned by Nate Williams and Tomas Markovic}}{\text{Total points earned by Hal Jackson}}$

5. $\dfrac{\text{Total points earned by Lukas Novak and Bobby Chow}}{\text{Total points earned by Nate Williams and Tomas Markovic}}$

6. $\dfrac{\text{Total points earned by Hal Jackson}}{\text{Total points earned by Lukas Novak and Bobby Chow}}$

Number sense

Name _____

Percentage of Price Increase and Decrease

Example

If the price of a basketball jersey increased from $48 to $64, what is the percentage of price increase?

$$\frac{\text{Change in Price}}{\text{Original Price}} = \frac{16}{48} = .3333 = 33.3\% \text{ increase}$$

1. If the price of an autographed basketball increases from $185 to $325, what is the percentage of price increase?

2. If the price of a basketball video game decreases from $95 to $88, what is the percentage of price decrease?

3. If the price of a season ticket decreases from $8,200 to $7,900, what is the percentage of price decrease?

4. If the price of a season ticket increases from $465 to $770, what is the percentage of price increase?

5. If a salary cap increases from $25 million to $30.5 million, what percentage increase would that represent?

Number sense

Finding a Percentage of a Number

Example

Rachel Allen earned $\frac{17}{36}$ point while Zi Yu earned $\frac{1}{2}$ point. What percentage of Yu's points do Allen's points represent?

$$\frac{17}{36} = n \times \frac{1}{2}$$

$$\text{therefore, } n = \frac{17}{36} \div \frac{1}{2}$$

$$\text{thus, } n = \frac{17}{36} \times \frac{2}{1} = \frac{34}{36} = .9\overline{4} = 94.4\%$$

1. Alice Jackson earned $\frac{19}{36}$ point while Wilma Wilford earned $\frac{1}{4}$ point. What percentage of Wilford's points do Jackson's points represent?

2. Hosanna Brown earned $\frac{1}{6}$ point while Teri Corelly earned $\frac{2}{9}$ point. What percentage of Corelly's points do Brown's points represent?

3. Danielle Miller earned $\frac{1}{3}$ point while Erika Jansson earned $\frac{13}{26}$ point. What percentage of Miller's points do Jansson's points represent?

4. Jada Hughes earned $\frac{7}{36}$ point, which was 700% of Yin Feng's points. How many points did Feng earn?

Number sense

Finding a Percentage
of a Number *(Cont'd.)*

5. Donna Klaus earned $\frac{12}{36}$ point, which was 120% of Sondi Carter's points. How many points did Carter earn?

6. If Lashawna Jones earned 150% of her week 8 point total of $\frac{12}{36}$, how many points did she earn?

7. There are two million Buzz fans in New York and one million Swarm fans in New Jersey. Each year, .02 of the Buzz fans move to New Jersey and .25 of the Swarm fans move to New York. Complete the table below.

After Year	Buzz Fans in New York	Swarm Fans in New Jersey
1		
2		
3		
4		

Number sense

Proportions

Example

If Joy Bryant earned $1.\overline{3}$ points during the first four games of the season, how many points is she projected to earn for an entire 82-game season?

$$\frac{1.\overline{3}}{4} = \frac{n}{82} \qquad\qquad 1.\overline{3}\,(82) = 4n \qquad\qquad n = 27.\overline{3}$$

1. If Carmita Martinez earned $10\frac{9}{36}$ points during the first 41 games of the season, how many points is she projected to earn for the entire 82-game season?

2. If it took Jessica Allen three games to earn $\frac{21}{36}$ point, how many games would it take her to earn $1\frac{20}{36}$ points?

3. If it took Steve McNally 12 games to earn 4 points, how many games would it take him to earn 6 points?

4. Willie Poole earned $22\frac{28}{36}$ points for the entire season. If he earned an equal number of points each game, how many points would he have earned after nine games?

5. Lukas Novak earned 41 points for an 82-game season. If he earned an equal amount of points each game, how many points would he have earned after seven games?

Number sense 153

Proportions *(Cont'd.)*

6. If Bonita Garcia made 25 free throws during the first five games, how many free throws is she projected to make for an 82-game season?

7. Mo Montclair made six three-point shots during the first 3 games. If he maintains his current pace, how many three-point shots will he make during the first 24 games?

8. An architect is constructing a scale drawing of a new arena. On the scale, one inch represents two feet. If the actual length of a basketball court is 94 feet, then what is the length of the court in the scale drawing?

9. In problem 8, what is the width of the court if its width in the scale drawing is 25 inches?

10. If it took 35 hours to drive 1,800 miles nonstop, how long would it take to drive 3,000 miles nonstop, assuming that the average speed would remain constant on both trips?

Number sense

Name _____

Ratios and Proportions

Example

During week 4, the ratio of Ty Jackson's points to YoLanda Williams's points was 3:1. If Jackson earned $\frac{21}{36}$ point that week, how many points did Williams earn?

$$\frac{3}{1} = \frac{.58\overline{3}}{n}$$

$$3n = 1(.58\overline{3})$$

$$n = .19\overline{4}$$

1. During week 14, the ratio of Isiah Smith's points to Hanna Blade's points was 4:3. If Blade earned $\frac{9}{36}$ point that week, how many points did Smith earn?

2. During week 12, the ratio of Bobby Chow's points to Loren Grattis's points was 1:3. If Grattis earned $\frac{27}{36}$ point that week, how many points did Chow earn?

3. During week 13, the ratio of Derek Jones's points to Brianna Fisher's points was 5:2. If Jones earned $\frac{25}{36}$ point that week, how many points did Fisher earn?

4. During week 14, the ratio of Lukas Novak's points to Tyceen Davis's points was 6:5. If Davis earned $\frac{15}{36}$ point that week, how many points did Novak earn?

Number sense

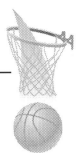

PRACTICE WORKSHEET 21

Factoring

Example

Jamaal Crow earned $\frac{18}{36}$ point during week 8. If one factor of $\frac{18}{36}$ is $\frac{3}{12}$, what is the second factor?

$$\frac{3}{12} \times n = \frac{18}{36}$$

$$n = \frac{6}{3} = 2$$

1. The product of the points earned by Jason Crawford and Sal Stein for week 8 is $\frac{2}{18}$. If Stein earned $\frac{1}{2}$ point, how many points did Crawford earn?

2. Find two factors (other than 1) whose product equals $1\frac{12}{36}$.

3. The area of a table tennis table is 32 square feet. If the length and width are whole numbers, what are the only two realistic factors for the table's dimensions?

4. Beverly Dallas earned $\frac{12}{36}$ point and $\frac{2}{9}$ point in consecutive weeks. What is the product of her points earned?

Number sense

PRACTICE WORKSHEET 22

Interest, Depreciation, and Tax

1. Assume that a player signed an eight-year contract for $145,000,000 and that his income remains constant during the life of the contract. If the player invests 35% of his yearly salary at a rate of 6.25%, how much interest will he earn at the end of two years if the interest is compounded annually? Construct a table showing the interest earned and total value of his account at the end of each year. Use the following formula:

   $I = PRT$
   $I =$ interest earned
   $P =$ principle
   $R =$ interest rate
   $T =$ time

2. If Tom Galland purchased a car for $180,000 and the state sales tax rate was 8.5%, how much tax did he pay? What was the total cost of the car?

3. If the value of the automobile in problem 2 depreciates by 10% each year, what will the car be worth at the end of three years? Construct a table showing the amount of depreciation and the corresponding value of the car each year.

4. A player purchases a house for $6,500,000. If the price of the home appreciates 10% a year for the next two years, what will be the value of the home at the end of that period? Construct a table showing the amount of annual appreciation and the corresponding value of the house at the end of each year.

Name _____

Prime Factorization

1. Below are the weekly point totals (in 36ths) for the Huskies for weeks 1–6. Use exponents to write the prime factorization of each number.

Week	*Point Totals*	*Prime Factorization*
Week 1	32	2^5
Week 2	39	
Week 3	72	
Week 4	49	
Week 5	62	
Week 6	29	

2. List the first five prime numbers: _____ _____ _____ _____ _____

Number sense

Name _____

Scientific Notation

Example

The dimensions of a basketball court are 94 feet by 50 feet. Write the area of the court in square feet, using scientific notation.

$$Area = 94 \times 50 = 4{,}700 \text{ sq. feet} = 4.7 \times 10^3$$

Write the area of the court in the following units, using scientific notation.

1. Square inches:

2. Square yards:

Write the following in scientific notation.

3. 928.75

4. .20005

5. .0999997

6. 304,887.5665

7. 5,005,005.555

Write the following in standard form.

8. 3.552×10^{-4}

9. $\dfrac{2}{9} \times 10^5$

Number sense

PRACTICE WORKSHEET 25

Ordering Integers, Fractions, and Decimals

1. The following integers represent temperatures in December for several cities that host basketball teams. Place them on the number line below in ascending order.

42   −31   −21   −5   −11   −32   21   66   48   −4   56

2. The following point values were earned by Bobby Chow, using a scoring system that is based on negative numerical values. Place them on the number line below in ascending order.

$$-\frac{1}{3} \quad -\frac{3}{16} \quad -\frac{5}{36} \quad -\frac{17}{48} \quad -\frac{1}{6} \quad -\frac{5}{8} \quad -\frac{5}{12}$$

3. Place the points earned by the players on the Huskies for the first two games (shown below) on the following number line in ascending order.

.37   −.345   −.656   −.199   .773   .802   .505   −.565   .565

Number sense

PRACTICE WORKSHEET 26
Operations with Integers

1. If Tre Williams earned −1230 points for turnovers and personal fouls over the course of 15 seasons, how many average points per season did he earn for turnovers and personal fouls?

2. The integers below represent the points earned by 10 players on a team. What is the sum of the points earned by the team?

   −9   −31   −22   19   18   −22   −4   −5   −33   23

3. If Jack Blue earned −7 points for the first game of the season, how many points is he projected to earn for an 82-game season?

4. If Shantaya Holmes earned −3 points for the first game of the season, how many points is she projected to earn for the first 58 games?

Number sense

Operations with Integers *(Cont'd.)*

5. The numbers below represent profit or loss for five teams for one year. What is the average profit or loss?

$-$825,000 $5,087,435 $-$3,000,256 $-$84,773 $15,004,232

6. In 2004, one team lost $1,878,330 while another team reported a profit of $13,656,950. How much greater was the second team's profit than the other team's loss?

7. A team reported a loss of $2,111,008, which included a profit of $1,777,456 on parking fees. How much money did the team lose on operations other than the parking fees?

Name _____

Permutations and Combinations

1. There are six guards on a team. If the coach starts two guards, how many combinations can he choose from?

2. If a team has jerseys in three different styles, shoes in two different styles, and pants in three different styles, how many combinations of uniforms do they have to choose from?

3. A team's uniform consists of two colors, but they have five colors to choose from. How many combinations of uniforms do they have?

4. Before a game, 12 players from one team line up in single file for the National Anthem. In how many ways can they line up in single file?

Number sense

Unit Conversions

1. The length of a basketball court is 94 feet. What is the length of the court in inches? In centimeters? (2.5 centimeters = 1 inch)

2. The rim of the basket is 10 feet above the floor. How many inches is the rim above the floor?

3. The width of a basketball court is 50 feet. What is the width of the court in yards?

4. If the length of a court is 1,128 inches, what is the length of the court in millimeters? *Hint:* 10 mm = 1 cm

5. A team spent 2,200 minutes practicing last week. How many hours did they spend practicing last week?

6. A team is scheduled to play their next game in exactly 2 days, 17 hours. How many hours will pass before they play their next game? How many minutes?

Algebra and functions

PRACTICE WORKSHEET 29
Evaluating Algebraic Expressions

Evaluate $\dfrac{1}{36}(P) + \dfrac{1}{9}(R) + \dfrac{1}{6}(B) + \dfrac{1}{12}(A + S) - \dfrac{1}{18}(T + F)$ if

1. $P = 2$
    $R = 3$
    $B = 1$
    $A = 3$
    $S = 1$
    $T = 2$
    $F = 1$

2. $P = 4$
    $R = 3$
    $B = 2$
    $A = 1$
    $S = 3$
    $T = 2$
    $F = 0$

Evaluate $\left(\dfrac{W}{S}\right)360$ if

3. $W = \dfrac{17}{36}$

    $S = 1\dfrac{2}{9}$

4. $W = \dfrac{1}{2}$

    $S = 2\dfrac{1}{2}$

Algebra and functions

Properties of Mathematics

Examples

Distributive property	$a(b + c) = ab + ac$
Commutative property of addition	$a + b = b + a$
Commutative property of multiplication	$ab = ba$
Associative property of addition	$a + (b + c) = (a + b) + c$
Associative property of multiplication	$a(bc) = (ab)c$
Inverse property of addition	$a + (-a) = 0$
Inverse property of multiplication	$a \times \dfrac{1}{a} = 1$
Identity property of addition	$a + 0 = a$
Identity property of multiplication	$a(1) = a$

The following equations are used to compute the points earned in various fantasy sports. List the mathematical property of each, and fill in the missing term.

1. $\dfrac{1}{36} \times$ _____ $= \dfrac{1}{36}$

   Property: _____

2. $\dfrac{1}{2} R \times \dfrac{7}{9} C = \dfrac{7}{9} C \times$ _____

   Property: _____

Algebra and functions

Properties of Mathematics *(Cont'd.)*

3. $\frac{13}{36}\left(P + \frac{1}{2}\right) = \frac{13}{36}P + $ _____

   Property: _____

4. $\frac{25}{36}R + \left(\frac{1}{2}C + \frac{2}{5}P\right) = \left(\frac{25}{36}R + \rule{2cm}{0.4pt}\right) + \frac{2}{5}P$

   Property: _____

5. $\frac{3}{10}P \times \left(\frac{19}{36}C \times \frac{2}{9}R\right) = \left(\rule{2cm}{0.4pt} \times \frac{19}{36}C\right) \times \frac{2}{9}R$

   Property: _____

6. $\frac{4}{9}C + $ _____ $= 0$

   Property: _____

7. $\frac{7}{8} \times$ _____ $= 1$

   Property: _____

8. $7\frac{1}{2} + $ _____ $= 7\frac{1}{2}$

   Property: _____

9. _____ $(1) = \frac{31}{48}$

   Property: _____

PRACTICE WORKSHEET 31

Graphing on a Number Line

(Use with Handout 12)

Example

During the first six weeks, Bobby Chow's range of points earned was between $\frac{20}{36}$ and $\frac{9}{36}$, inclusive. From these data, we can graph Chow's range of points earned on a number line.

$$\frac{20}{36} \qquad \frac{9}{36}$$

Use a number line to graph the range of points earned in weeks 1–6 for the following players:

1. Lukas Novak   _____

2. Nate Williams   _____

3. Tomas Markovic   _____

4. Hal Jackson   _____

Algebra and functions

Name _____

Linear Equations (A)

The equations below are used to compute total weekly points or to compute central angles in a circle graph. In each case, solve for the variable.

1. $\dfrac{1}{36}(P) + \dfrac{1}{9}(1) + \dfrac{1}{6}(0) + \dfrac{1}{12}(2) - \dfrac{1}{18}(1) = \dfrac{11}{36}$

2. $.6^0(5) + .6^{-1}(2) + .6^{-2}(B) + .6^{-3}(0) - .6^{-4}(1) = 6.017\overline{3}$

3. $2^1(6) + 2^2(R) + 2^3(1) + 2^4(4) - 2^5(1) = 64$

4. $\left(\displaystyle\sum_{j=1}^{6} j\right)(1) + \left(\displaystyle\sum_{j=1}^{5} j\right)(0) + \left(\displaystyle\sum_{j=1}^{4} j\right)(2) + \left(\displaystyle\sum_{j=1}^{3} j\right)(A + 2) - \left(\displaystyle\sum_{j=1}^{2} j\right)(1) = 20$

Algebra and functions

Linear Equations (A) *(Cont'd.)*

5. $W \div 1\frac{1}{4} \times 360 = 180$

6. $\frac{5}{8}(P) + \frac{4}{5}(0) + \frac{3}{4}(1) + .3(1) - \frac{2}{8}(0) = 2.3$

7. $.075(2) + \frac{1}{40}(1) + .0125(1) + \frac{1}{20}(A + 0) - .0375(2) = .2625$

8. $\left(\frac{5}{6}\right)^0(P) + \left(\frac{4}{5}\right)^1(1) + \left(\frac{3}{4}\right)^2(2) + \left(\frac{2}{7}\right)^3(0) - \left(\frac{2}{8}\right)^0(2) = 4.9259$

9. $-6^0(7) - 6^1(2) - 6^2(1) - 6^3(3 + 2) + 6^4(3 + F) = 7{,}937$

Algebra and functions

Linear Equations (A) *(Cont'd.)*

10. $\left(\dfrac{1}{4}\right)^{0}(3) + \left(\dfrac{1}{4}\right)^{-1}(4) + \left(\dfrac{1}{4}\right)^{-2}(B) + \left(\dfrac{1}{4}\right)^{-3}(0 + 5) - \left(\dfrac{1}{4}\right)^{-4}(2 + 4) = -1165$

11. $.3^{0}(0) + .3^{1}(R) + .3^{2}(0) + .3^{3}(0 + 0) - .3^{4}(1 + 4) = -.0405$

12. $2^{0}(8) + 2^{-1}(2) + 2^{-2}(2) + 2^{-3}(3 + 1) - 2^{-4}(T + 4) = 10.625$

13. $\sqrt{121}(1) + \sqrt{100}(5) + \sqrt{81}(4) + \sqrt{64}(A + 2) - \sqrt{49}(4 + 3) = 88$

Algebra and functions

Linear Equations (A) *(Cont'd.)*

14. $4^4 (3) + 4^3 (3) + 4^2 (3) + 4^1 (3 + S) - 4^0 (3 + 3) = 1022$

15. $-5^4 (1) - 5^3 (R) - 5^2 (3) - 5^1 (0 + 1) + 5^0 (2 + 2) = 49$

16. $\left(\dfrac{1}{2}\right)^{-2} (P) + \sqrt[3]{64}(1) + 025(0) + \left(\dfrac{2}{8}\right)^{\circ} (1 + 1) - 2^{-3}(4 + 4) = 18$

Algebra and functions

Name _____

Linear Equations (B)

In the problems below, insert the values shown for each variable in the total points equation. Then solve for W and write the answer in its simplest form.

$$\frac{1}{36}(P) + \frac{1}{9}(R) + \frac{1}{6}(B) + \frac{1}{12}(A + S) - \frac{1}{18}(T + F) = W$$

1. $P = 5$
   $R = 2$
   $B = 2$
   $A = 3$
   $S = 1$
   $T = 2$
   $F = 1$

2. $P = 2$
   $R = 1$
   $B = 3$
   $A = 2$
   $S = 0$
   $T = 1$
   $F = 3$

3. $P = 3$
   $R = 0$
   $B = 1$
   $A = 2$
   $S = 2$
   $T = 0$
   $F = 4$

Algebra and functions

PRACTICE WORKSHEET 34

Area and Perimeter of Rectangles

1. Explain the meaning of the variables in the following equations:

   $P = 2l + 2w$

   $A = bh$

2. The dimensions of a professional basketball court are 94 feet by 50 feet. The length and width of a high school court are 84 feet by 50 feet. Find the area of both playing surfaces in the following units of measurement. Then find the ratio of the area of the professional court to the area of the high school court in each measurement unit. Do you see any patterns? Explain.

	Area of Professional Basketball Court	Area of High School Basketball Court	Ratio of Area of Professional Basketball Court to Area of High School Basketball Court
Square feet			
Square inches			
Square yards			
Square centimeters (2.5 cm = 1 inch)			
Square millimeters			
Square meters			

Measurement and geometry

Area and Perimeter of Rectangles

(Cont'd.)

3. If a professional court costs $225 per square foot, how much would it cost to replace the entire floor of the court?

4. How much more would it cost to replace a professional floor than a high school floor?

5. Consider the playing surfaces listed below, then make two statements comparing their sizes. For example, you may predict that a football field is three times larger than a basketball court or that a soccer field is 15% larger than a rugby field. Then find the actual area and see how close your predictions were. Finally, find the perimeter of each area.

Statement 1:

Statement 2:

Playing Area	Dimensions	Area	Perimeter
Football field	300 ft. by 160 ft.		
Soccer field	68 m. by 105 m.		
Professional basketball court	94 ft. by 50 ft.		
High school basketball court	84 ft. by 50 ft.		

Golden Rectangles

1. The ratio of length to width in a Golden Rectangle is approximately 1.6:1.
   Fill in the table below:

	Dimensions	Ratio of Length to Width	Difference from Golden Rectangle Ratio
Basketball court	94 ft. by 50 ft.		
Horse racing track facility	2,640 ft. by 1,320 ft.		
Middle school basketball court	70 ft. by 40 ft.		
Race car track facility	2.5 miles by 1.75 miles		
Junior high basketball court	74 ft. by 42 ft.		

2. In the preceding table, which playing surfaces or facilities have a ratio that approximates that of a Golden Rectangle?

3. Measure the length and width of various objects to find examples of Golden Rectangles. Some suggestions: flags, calculators, books, blackboards, windows, doors, file cabinets.

4. Predict the ratio of your height to the span of your two arms. Find the ratio. What did you learn?

Measurement and geometry

Name _____

PRACTICE WORKSHEET 36

Functions

In each of the following exercises, write the function rule and solve for the variable.

1. X = number of rebounds in sets of 5; Y = points earned

Function rule: _____

X	Y
1	$\frac{1}{9}$
2	$\frac{2}{9}$
3	n
7	$\frac{4}{9}$

2. X = number of blocked shots in sets of 3; Y = points earned

Function rule: _____

X	Y
4	n
3	$\frac{3}{6}$
2	$\frac{2}{6}$
1	$\frac{1}{6}$

Measurement and geometry

177

Functions *(Cont'd.)*

3. X = number of points scored in sets of 5; Y = points earned

Function rule: _____

X	Y
3	$\dfrac{3}{36}$
4	$\dfrac{4}{36}$
5	n
7	$\dfrac{7}{36}$

4. Below, construct your own function chart. Let X = number of assists and steals in sets of 3 and Y = points earned.

Function rule: _____

X	Y

Measurement and geometry

PRACTICE WORKSHEET 37

Area and Circumference
of Circles

Area of a circle = πr^2

Circumference of a circle = πd

r = radius; d = diameter; π = 3.14

1. A circular logo at the center of a basketball court has a diameter of 12 feet. Find the area and circumference of the logo.

2. If the area of a circular logo is 78.5 square feet, what is the diameter of the logo?

3. A circular logo on a high school basketball court has a diameter of 9 feet. What is the area of the logo?

4. If the logo at the center of a basketball court has a radius of 4 feet, what are the diameter, circumference, and area of the circle?

Diameter: _____

Circumference: _____

Area: _____

5. If the circumference of a circular logo on a shirt is 9.42 inches, what are the radius, diameter, and area of the logo?

Radius: _____

Diameter: _____

Area: _____

Name _____

Weight

1. Predict, then find, the weight of the following objects, in the given units. You will need a scale.

	Predicted Weight			Actual Weight		
	Pounds	Ounces	Grams	Pounds	Ounces	Grams
Football						
Basketball						
Baseball						
Soccer ball						
Table tennis ball						
Hockey puck						

For each of the following problems, predict the answer, then solve the problem.

2. How many table tennis balls would weigh as much as a basketball? As much as a soccer ball?

3. Which is greater, the weight of two hockey pucks or six basketballs?

4. How many basketballs would it take to equal your body weight? How many hockey pucks? Table tennis balls?

Measurement and geometry

Name _____

The Pythagorean Theorem

$$a^2 + b^2 = c^2$$

where

    a = length of one leg of the triangle
    b = length of the other leg of the triangle
    c = length of the hypotenuse

Use the Pythagorean Theorem to solve the following problems:

1. Find the length of the diagonal of a high school basketball court if the length of the court is 84 feet and the width is 45 feet.

2. Find the length of the diagonal of a horse racing facility if the length of the facility is 2,600 feet and the width is 1,320 feet.

3. Find the length of the diagonal of one-half of the length of a basketball court if the length of the entire court is 94 feet and the width is 50 feet.

4. Find the width of a soccer field if the length of the field is 35 meters and the length of its diagonal is 52 meters.

5. The length of a lacrosse field is 125 yards, and the length of its diagonal is 185 yards. Find the width of the field.

Measurement and geometry

Mean, Median, Mode, Range

(Use with Handout 12)

Example

Find the mean, median, mode, and range of the points earned by the players on the Huskies for week 5.

Mean: $1\dfrac{26}{36} \div 5 = .3\overline{4}$

Median: $\dfrac{2}{36} \quad \dfrac{7}{36} \quad \dfrac{12}{36} \quad \dfrac{20}{36} \quad \dfrac{21}{36} = \dfrac{12}{36}$

Mode: None

Range: $\dfrac{21}{36} - \dfrac{2}{36} = \dfrac{19}{36}$

1. For each of the first three weeks, find the points earned by each player on the Huskies. In the table below, record the mean, median, mode, and range of those points for each week.

Week	Mean	Median	Mode	Range
1				
2				
3				

2. For each of the first five weeks, find the points earned by each player on your starting team. In the table below, record the mean, median, mode, and range of those points for each of the first five weeks.

Week	Mean	Median	Mode	Range
1				
2				
3				
4				
5				

Statistics, data analysis, and probability

Probability

1. Last year, 25% of Jessie Robinson's field goal attempts came from the left side of the court, 35% came from the right side of the court, and 40% came from the middle of the court. If Robinson had 2,000 field goal attempts last year, how many shots did she attempt from each direction?

2. Using only the data in problem 1, what is the probability that Robinson's first field goal attempt this year will be from the left side of the court?

3. A team's record during the last 10 years is 500–320. Without taking any other variables into account, what should the team's record be this year?

4. The probability of a team winning a game is 50%. Express the outcome in several other ways. *Hint:* $\frac{1}{2}$

5. If the probability of Kevin Oliphant making a field goal is 55%, what is the probability that he will miss the shot?

Statistics, data analysis, and probability

Probability *(Cont'd.)*

6. The letters in "Dranusy Zikslagus" are placed in a hat. Find the probability of the following random events:

   A. Selecting the letter *g*

   B. Selecting the letters *z, a,* or *r*

   C. Selecting the letter *s*

   D. Selecting any letter except *r*

   E. Selecting the letter *g*, replacing it, then selecting the letter *g* again

   F. Selecting the letters *d* and *k* on consecutive draws (without replacing letters)

In exercises 7–11, you are given $P(Q)$, the probability that Lisa Ming will block 3 shots in a given game. Find $P(\text{not } Q)$, the probability that event Q will not occur.

7. $P(Q) = \dfrac{4}{9}$ $P(\text{not } Q) =$

8. $P(Q) = .525$ $P(\text{not } Q) =$

9. $P(Q) = 17\%$ $P(\text{not } Q) =$

10. $P(Q) = 1$ $P(\text{not } Q) =$

11. $P(Q) = 0$ $P(\text{not } Q) =$

Statistics, data analysis, and probability

Name _____

PRACTICE WORKSHEET 42
Circle Graphs

(Use with Handout 12)

$W \div S \times 360 = A$

W = total weekly points for one player
S = total weekly points for the team
A = central angle of the circle graph

Example

In week 2, Joe Washington earned $\frac{1}{6}$ point. Find the measurement of the central angle in a circle graph (to the nearest tenth) representing Washington's contribution to his team's total points for that week.

$$\frac{1}{6} \div \frac{39}{36} \times 360 = 55.38 = 55.4 \text{ degrees}$$

1. Find the central angles for all players on the Huskies for week 2. Then construct a circle graph.

2. Find the central angles for all players on the Huskies for week 5. Then construct a circle graph.

3. Construct a circle graph showing the central angle measurements for the cumulative scoring breakdown for the players on the Huskies for weeks 1–6.

4. If the central angle in a circle graph is 15 degrees, what percentage of the graph will that section represent?

5. If the central angle in a circle graph is 190 degrees, what percentage of the graph will that section represent?

6. If one section of a circle graph represents 65% of the total graph, what is the measurement of the corresponding central angle?

7. The sum of the central angles inside a circle graph is 359 degrees. Explain how this could occur.

Statistics, data analysis, and probability   185

Name _____

Stem-and-Leaf Plots and Histograms

1. The following values represent the point totals (in 36ths) for the Huskies for the first 16 games of the season. Using graph paper, construct a stem-and-leaf plot and a histogram based on the data.

| 86 | 79 | 38 | 50 | 88 | 66 | 69 | 120 |
| 94 | 88 | 85 | 77 | 70 | 49 | 100 | 95 |

2. The following values represent the point totals (in 36ths) for Barbara Washington for the first 16 games of the season. Using graph paper, construct a stem-and-leaf plot and a histogram based on the data.

| 19 | 9 | 17 | 21 | 12 | 14 | 8 | 31 |
| 41 | 26 | 34 | 29 | 4 | 10 | 16 | 37 |

Statistics, data analysis, and probability

PRACTICE WORKSHEET 44

Scatter Plots

1. The table below represents hypothetical ticket prices from 1990 to 1999. On graph paper, construct a scatter plot of these data. Does the scatter plot show a positive or negative correlation? Explain.

Year	Average Price per Ticket
1990	$42.50
1991	$44.87
1992	$48.57
1993	$50.25
1994	$52.56
1995	$55.79
1996	$57.03
1997	$61.11
1998	$63.66
1999	$65.74

2. The table below shows the height of various players and the number of rebounds they got in one year. Using graph paper, construct a scatter plot of these data. Does the scatter plot show a positive or negative correlation? Explain.

Player	Player's Height	Number of Rebounds
A	6'3"	313
B	6'7"	437
C	5'10"	242
D	6'4"	422
E	6'10"	729
F	7'5"	806
G	6'1"	199

Statistics, data analysis, and probability

Name _____

Box-and-Whisker Plots

The following data sets represent the points earned (in 36ths) by Bobby Chow and the total team points earned by the Huskies for the last twelve weeks of the season. Draw a box-and-whisker plot for each set of data. On each plot, label the median as well as the upper and lower quartiles.

1. Bobby Chow   23, 9, 17, 21, 12, 10, 8, 31, 37, 42, 35, 18

2. The Huskies   66, 79, 38, 50, 106, 66, 69, 111, 49, 100, 95, 81

Statistics, data analysis, and probability

PRACTICE WORKSHEET 46

Statements Using Math Terminology

(Use with Handout 12)

Statements are complete sentences based on a set of data. Statements must be accompanied by mathematical proof. The statements on this worksheet were derived from Handout 12.

Example

In week 2, Hal Jackson earned one-half as many points as Bobby Chow earned.

$$\text{Proof:} \quad \frac{1}{2} \text{ of } \frac{12}{36} = \frac{6}{36}$$

For the following statements, show mathematical proof.

1. In week 2, the guards earned fewer points than the forwards.

2. In week 2, Bobby Chow and Lukas Novak accounted for over 58% of the total points earned.

3. In week 2, Tomas Markovic accounted for approximately 8% of his team's total points.

4. In week 2, Bobby Chow earned $\frac{1}{18}$ more points than the guards earned.

5. In week 2, Bobby Chow and Lukas Novak earned $\frac{7}{36}$ more points than Hal Jackson, Nate Williams, and Tomas Markovic.

6. Using the information from Handout 12, write five statements and show mathematical proof.

   A.

   B.

   C.

   D.

   E.

Mathematical reasoning

189

Extra Credit Problems

1. A ball was dropped from the top of a building that is 150 feet high. Each time the basketball bounces, it rebounds to 65% of its height on the previous rebound. On which bounce does the ball bounce less than one foot high?

2. A. Find the arena seating capacity, average ticket price, and revenue for two professional basketball teams. Revenue is defined as the number of tickets sold multiplied by the average price of a ticket, multiplied by 41 (the number of regular-season home games each team plays during one season).

   B. What is the difference in revenue between the two teams for one game? For one season?

   C. How much would revenue increase (for one game) for one of the teams if they increased ticket prices by an average of 5%?

   D. How much would revenue decrease (for the season) for one of the teams if they decreased ticket prices by an average of 3%?

3. Create a new scoring system, using fractions, decimals, factorials, summations, exponents, roots, or a mixture of all of the above. Then compute your current weekly and cumulative points using that scoring system.

Assessment

Name _____

Pretest/Posttest

Show all of your work.

1. Find the sum of the points earned by the following players:

   Nate Williams $\dfrac{29}{36}$

   Tomas Markovic $\dfrac{2}{3}$

   Lukas Novak $\dfrac{5}{6}$

   Bobby Chow $\dfrac{7}{12}$

2. In problem 1, what is the ratio of the points earned by Tomas Markovic to the points earned by Lukas Novak?

3. In problem 1, convert Markovic's points to a decimal and round to the nearest thousandth.

4. Evaluate

   $$\frac{1}{36}\,(P) + \frac{1}{9}\,(R) + \frac{1}{6}\,(B) + \frac{1}{12}\,(A + S) - \frac{1}{18}\,(T + F) \text{ if}$$

   $P = 7$
   $R = 2$
   $B = 1$
   $A = 5$
   $S = 2$
   $T = 4$
   $F = 4$

Copyright © 2007 by Dan Flockhart

Assessment   193

Pretest/Posttest *(Cont'd.)*

5. If one factor of $\frac{18}{36}$ is $\frac{3}{9}$, what is the second factor?

6. Write the prime factorization of 72, using exponents.

7. Convert $\frac{58}{36}$ into a mixed number, and write it in the simplest form.

8. Which is the greater scoring average per game: 248 points for 12 games or 496 points for 24 games?

9. If a player accumulated $1\frac{2}{9}$ points during the first two games of the season, how many points is he projected to earn for 12 games?

Assessment

Pretest/Posttest *(Cont'd.)*

10. Based on the points earned by the players in problem 1, find the following:

    Range:

    Mean:

    Median:

    Mode:

11. Fill in the missing numbers in the patterns below.

    A. $\dfrac{5}{36}$ $\dfrac{5}{18}$ $\dfrac{5}{12}$ _____

    B. $\dfrac{2}{3}$ $1\dfrac{1}{3}$ 2 _____

12. The price of an autographed jersey rose from \$135 to \$190. Find the percentage of price increase.

13. If a player invests 30% of his annual salary of \$8.5 million at 7.5%, how much interest will he earn after one year?

14. A player has a gym at his house. The dimensions of the gym are 105 feet by 195 feet. Find the area of the gym in square inches.

15. In problem 14, what is the length of the diagonal of the gym?

Pretest/Posttest *(Cont'd.)*

16. The letters in "Stanley Walker" are placed in a hat. Find the probability of the following random events:

    A. Selecting the letter a

    B. Selecting the letters p, l, or e

17. Solve for the variable in the following equation:

    $$\frac{1}{36}(2) + \frac{1}{9}(2) + \frac{1}{6}(2) + \frac{1}{12}(4 + S) - \frac{1}{18}(3 + 5) = 18.5$$

Assessment